updated edition

A Ranger's Guide to
Yellowstone
Day Hikes

by Roger Anderson
and Carol Shively Anderson

FARCOUNTRY
PRESS

Acknowledgments

No one, despite the depth of their experience, can write a book on a place as vast as Yellowstone alone. We'd like to express our appreciation to our family, friends, and fellow park rangers for lending their expertise to this effort and for going the extra mile with us. Special regards go to Guida Veronda, who reviewed every mile of every trail in this book. Many thanks also to Jeanne Johnson, Bob Fuhrmann, Jon Dahlheim, Karen McBee, Ellen Petrick-Underwood, Carren Stewart, Dan Reinhart, Lori Roberts, Tom Farrell, Neysa Dickey, John Lounsbury, Bundy Phillips, Les Inafuku, John Varley, Rick Anderson, Judy Anderson, Callie Shively, and Jan Smith.

We'd like to acknowledge park photographer Jim Peaco and Jo Suderman for providing valuable assistance in obtaining photos from the Yellowstone slide collection and National Park Service cartographer Megan Kealy for her map designs. Many of the historical quotes and insights in this book are from the definitive work by park historian Lee Whittlesey, *Wonderland Nomenclature: A History of the Place Names of Yellowstone National Park*.

We'd also like to recognize the folks at Farcountry Press: Kathy Springmeyer, Barbara Fifer, Bob Smith, Merle Guy, and Brad Hurd. Their considerable talents took this book from idea to reality.

Thanks also to Roger's aunt, Eleanor DiGiacomo, for her support along the way, and to Carol's grandmother, Jeanette Shively, for encouraging us to write about our experiences in Yellowstone.

We are deeply grateful to our parents, Margaret and David Shively and Phyllis and Richard Anderson, who brought us to Yellowstone as kids and have supported us on this lifetime journey.

To enjoy these hikes safely and comfortably, inquire at park visitor centers about current trail conditions, weather, and recent bear sightings before hiking. Use good judgment when choosing a trail and be aware of changing conditions during the day. The schematic maps in this book are based on United States Geological Survey (USGS) 7.5 minute quadrangles. If you'd like more detailed maps, see ordering information for USGS maps on page 6.

Photography by Roger Anderson.
Front cover: Grand Prismatic Spring in the Midway Geyser Basin. Photo by Jeff Vanuga.
Inset photo by Jeff Henry.

ISBN 10: 1-56037-157-9
ISBN 13: 978-1-56037-157-1

Text © 2000 Roger Anderson and Carol Shively Anderson
© 2000 Farcountry Press
Updated 2005

13 12 11 10 09   3 4 5 6

Invitation

We hear much today about how overcrowded our national parks have become and how difficult it is to enjoy them. The glorious truth of the matter is, if you're willing to go even a half mile from the road, you can still have Yellowstone almost to yourself. As the renowned naturalist John Muir encouraged on his visit to the park in 1885:

Walk away quietly in any direction,
and taste the freedom of the mountaineer!

With more than 35 years of combined experience as park rangers in Yellowstone, we'd like to help you do that. With this book as your companion, it will be as though you have a ranger naturalist as your guide on every trail.

We'd like to help you learn about the plants and animals you see along the way. We'd like to tell you about the stories locked in stone. We'd like to present you with evidence of the greatest powers on the face of the earth. We'd like to show you a place where all the grand forces of Nature are still at play. We'd like to share with you some of the impressions other explorers have had of this extraordinary place. We'd like you to experience something of the peace, the beauty, and the inspiration we have found here in the world's first national park.

So get your boots on. Let's go hiking.

Roger Anderson and Carol Shively Anderson

A thousand Yellowstone wonders are calling,
"Look up and down and round about you!"
—John Muir

Table of Contents

Lake Trails

Grant Trails

Old Faithful Trails

Madison/Norris Trails

Trail Map Legend

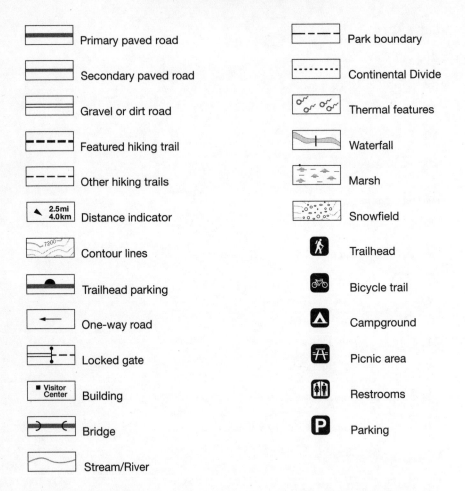

Primary paved road	Park boundary
Secondary paved road	Continental Divide
Gravel or dirt road	Thermal features
Featured hiking trail	Waterfall
Other hiking trails	Marsh
Distance indicator	Snowfield
Contour lines	Trailhead
Trailhead parking	Bicycle trail
One-way road	Campground
Locked gate	Picnic area
Building	Restrooms
Bridge	Parking
Stream/River	

Contour lines showing elevation gain on individual trail maps are to help you assess trail difficulty. Each contour line connects all points at the same elevation; numbers on the heavier lines state exact elevations in feet. The elevation interval between contour lines appears on each map—note that our maps use different intervals, depending on the trail. The closer together contour lines are, the steeper the trail's ascent or descent.

Refer to United States Geological Survey (USGS) maps for more detailed representations. They are sold in some outdoors stores; via mail from USGS Information Services, Box 25286, Denver, CO 80225 (phone 888-ASK-USGS); or see the USGS website at http://mapping.usgs.gov/mac/findmaps.html

Trail Locator Map

MAMMOTH HOT SPRINGS

TOWER-ROOSEVELT

LAMAR VALLEY

CANYON VILLAGE

NORRIS

MADISON

LAKE VILLAGE

YELLOWSTONE LAKE

OLD FAITHFUL

GRANT VILLAGE

SHOSHONE LAKE

Y E L L O W S T O N E   N A T I O N A L   P A R K

Choosing a Trail

Easy Hikes

Trail Number and Name	Area	Roundtrip Distance	Highlights	Page No.
1. Narrow Gauge Terrace	Mammoth	1.0mi/1.6km	Hot spring terraces	14
5. Yellowstone River Picnic Area	Tower	3.7mi/5.9km	Yellowstone River, "The Narrows" of the Canyon, rock formations	34
10. Trout Lake	Lamar	2.0mi/3.2km	Spawning trout, Trout Lake, mountain scenery	56
16. Pelican Creek	Lake	1.3mi/2.0km	Yellowstone Lake, Pelican Creek	86
17. Natural Bridge	Lake	3.0mi/4.8km	Natural bridge rock formation	90
18. Storm Point	Lake	2.3mi/3.7km	Indian Pond, Yellowstone Lake, rocky point	94
21. Lake Overlook	Grant	2.0mi/3.2km	Panoramic view of Yellowstone Lake	107
26. Mystic Falls	Old Faithful	2.0mi/3.2km	Sapphire Pool, 70' waterfall	129
28. Artists' Paintpots	Madison/Norris	1.0mi/1.6km	Mudpots	140

Moderate Hikes

Trail Number and Name	Area	Roundtrip Distance	Highlights	Page No.
2. Beaver Ponds	Mammoth	5.0mi/8.0km	Beaver ponds, aspen groves	18
3. The Hoodoos	Mammoth	3.0mi/4.8km	Rock formations	23
3. Snow Pass/Hoodoos Loop	Mammoth	6.2mi/10km	Mountain scenery, rock formations	23
6. Lost Lake	Tower	2.0mi/3.2km	40' waterfall, Lost Lake	38
6. Lost Lake/Petrified Tree Loop	Tower	3.5mi/5.6km	40' waterfall, Lost Lake, petrified tree	38
7. Slough Creek	Tower	4.0mi/6.4km	Slough Creek, meadows, mountain scenery, aspen groves	43
8. Hellroaring Creek	Tower	4.0mi/6.4km	Yellowstone River, suspension bridge, Hellroaring Creek	47
12. Cascade Lake	Canyon	5.0mi/8.0km	Cascade Lake, large meadows	65
13. South Rim of the Canyon	Canyon	4.5mi/7.2km	Grand Canyon, 109' & 308' waterfalls	70

*One-way distance; requires shuttle back to original trailhead

Trail Tips

What to Bring

Hiking in Yellowstone should be memorable for what you saw and experienced, not for what you forgot to bring that caused you discomfort. Don't start out on the trail without these few essentials:

1. Water; **2.** Sturdy hiking shoes; **3.** A hat and sunscreen; **4.** Raingear; **5.** Insect repellent

Bring water. Yellowstone has very low humidity. Even on a short hike, you can find yourself becoming dehydrated. Bring at least a quart of water—more for longer hikes. You'll want to be focusing on the beauty surrounding you, not on how incredibly thirsty you've suddenly become. Don't count on drinking water from the streams or lakes. Virtually all lakes and streams in the country are now affected by troublesome organisms and Yellowstone is no exception. The two primary suspects here are giardia lamblia and campylobactor. Both can cause mild to severe intestinal problems that occur after drinking the water (1-3 weeks for giardia and 3-5 days for campylobactor). These disorders are treatable, however. In case of emergency, to avoid serious dehydration, drink the water and be prepared to see a physician should any symptoms occur. On longer hikes, it's a good idea to bring some food or snacks along. Energy bars, fruit, and trail mix are good choices to keep your energy level high.

Wear sturdy hiking shoes. Because of both its volcanic and glacial past, Yellowstone is known for its rocky trails. You don't want to ruin your visit to the park with a sprained ankle or worse. Lightweight hiking shoes are adequate for the walks categorized as easy in this book, but heavier boots with good soles and ankle support are recommended for moderate and strenuous hikes.

Wear a hat and sunscreen. You'll be hiking at high elevation in Yellowstone. The cool mountain temperatures can be deceptive. Avoid at least a sunburn and at worst, heat exhaustion, by wearing a hat, for shade, and a strong sunscreen.

Carry raingear. Perhaps you've heard the old adage, "If you don't like the weather, just wait a minute, it will change." Because of Yellowstone's mountainous topography, what starts out as a beautiful clear day can turn into a cloudy downpour in minutes. Be prepared for the sudden change in the weather. In spring and fall when temperatures are colder, or when hiking at particularly high elevations any time of season, bring several layers of clothing to keep both warm and dry.

Bring insect repellent. Yellowstone's rich wetlands are a breeding ground for mosquitoes and several other biting insects. The park's general stores carry a variety of useful products to help prevent them from landing and biting.

What not to take. The national parks were established to preserve the natural and cultural heritage of the nation. Therefore, all natural and historic objects are protected by law. Don't take anything home as a souvenir of your visit to Yellowstone except great photographs and memories. This includes wildflowers, pine cones, rocks, petrified specimens, antlers, bones, skulls, and historic and prehistoric artifacts, including arrowheads.

There is an exception to this rule. You can pick nuts, berries, and mushrooms for your personal consumption only, not for commercial use. However, there have been fatalities in the park of people who didn't know which plants, berries, or mushrooms were poisonous. Don't experiment. Follow this simple rule, when in doubt, don't eat it!

Hiking in Bear Country

There is a great mystique that surrounds the grizzly bear—perhaps because it's so magnificent and yet so threatened. People come from all over the world to see bears in Yellowstone, and we hope you see them, too—from a safe distance. Here are some recommendations for hiking in bear country.

First and foremost, don't worry excessively about bears. Don't let this concern stop you from hiking. An encounter with either Yellowstone's black or grizzly bears is rare. Nonetheless, the potential danger involved warrants understanding a few simple concepts before starting out on the trail.

Just as there are no hard and fast rules that define bear behavior, there are no hard and fast rules to follow when you encounter a bear. There are a few suggestions, however, that might decrease the possibility of an incident.

Before you start hiking:
- Inquire at the visitor center or ranger station about recent bear sightings in the area.
- Check the trailhead for any current postings of bears on the trail.
- Don't hike alone. Hiking in groups of 4 or more is often recommended.
- Hike at mid-day. Don't hike at night, or at dawn and dusk, when bears are most active.

On the trail:
- Look for fresh scat (droppings). If you see it, choose another trail.

- Avoid carcasses. Bears will protect this important food source for themselves and their cubs.

- Look for bears. When approaching a blind curve or a hill, make noise—clap your hands, yell, or ring bear bells so you don't surprise a bear. (Ninety-seven percent of injuries due to bears in the last several decades occurred as the result of a surprise encounter.)

If you see a bear. If you see a bear from a distance (over 100 yards away) and it doesn't see you, walk away quietly. Save this hike for another day.

If you see a bear from a distance and it notices you, it may do nothing. Some bears have gotten quite accustomed to people. In this case, however, still walk away quietly. The bear could change its attitude in an instant. The bear may also run from you. If it continues to watch you, however, back away slowly. You could consider climbing a tree. But this should be done calmly and quietly, while there is still plenty of time to get 15-20 feet up the tree. Only attempt this if you are an experienced climber. Any quick movements could incite the bear to charge.

If a bear charges, don't run. Bears tend to chase anyone or anything that flees from them. Stand your ground. If it's a "bluff charge" the bear will stop short in front of you, then turn and walk away. Wait for it to leave the area.

If a bear attacks, play dead. Curl up on your stomach with your knees against your chest and your hands locked around your neck. Leave your pack on to protect your back. Don't yell or fight back. One theory is that the bear may perceive you as a threat to itself, its cubs, or a food source it's protecting. If you cease to be threatening by lying quiet and still, the bear will likely go away. Wait for it to leave before you make any further movements. Report any bear sightings or incidents to the nearest ranger station or visitor center.

Using pepper spray. Pepper spray has been found useful as a deterrent against bear attacks in some situations. However, results of studies done on its effectiveness are currently inconclusive. It has proven most successful when the hiker wears the canister in an easily accessible location and when he or she has practiced drawing the canister and removing the safety piece in a rapid and smooth motion.

Wildlife Etiquette

Park regulations require that you stay 25 yards away from wildlife, 100 yards away from bears. A good rule of thumb is, if an animal notices you, you're too close. Give them a wide berth on the trail. While elk, deer, bison, moose and other animals don't have the fearful reputation that bears do, they can still be quite dangerous. More injuries result from incidents with these animals than with bears. Though they are not known to be aggressive, they do require personal space and will protect their young. Be respectful. Keep your distance.

It is against the law to feed any wildlife in the park. This includes all animals, regardless of size, as well as birds and fish. While it may be tempting to feed animals to get a closer look at them, you wouldn't be doing them or yourself any favors. Animals who are fed become accustomed or "habituated" to humans. This may make them less likely to survive in the wild. Sometimes, they must be destroyed because of the personal injury or property damage they have done as a result of their unnatural association with people. They may also carry diseases such as rabies.

Enjoy all wildlife from a distance.

Lightning

Many of Yellowstone's trails afford extraordinary views from the tops of mountain peaks. This, however, also makes you vulnerable to lightning. Be aware of the changing weather. Lightning travels ahead of a storm. Take cover before it strikes. Follow these few simple guidelines to insure that your hike is an illuminating experience, mentally, not physically! If lightning is nearby:

◆ Get off of exposed ridges.

◆ Avoid solitary trees, rocks, lakes, or ponds, because they attract lightning.

◆ Take cover in the forest, if possible.

◆ If you can't find a forest for cover, crouch down low with only your boots touching the ground.

◆ Stay away from any objects that could conduct electricity, such as tripods, graphite fishing poles, frame packs, or metal tent poles.

◆ Don't group together with your hiking partners. If one person is hit, the others will need to go for help.

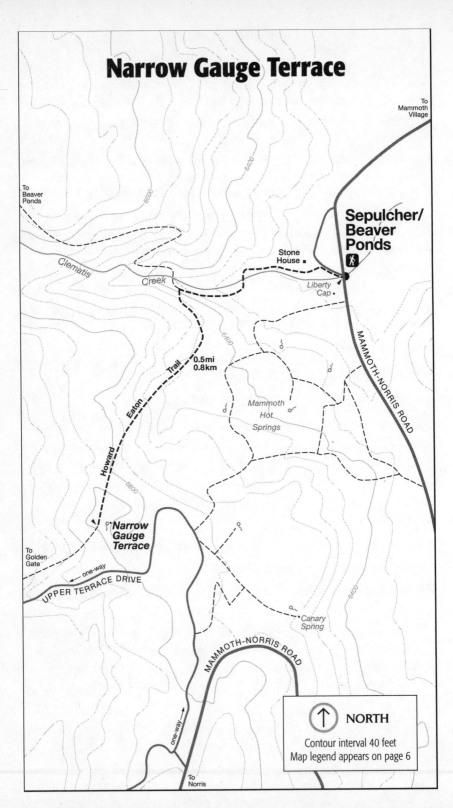

Narrow Gauge Terrace

To Mammoth Village

To Beaver Ponds

Sepulcher/ Beaver Ponds

Clematis

Creek

Stone House

Liberty Cap

Eaton Trail

0.5mi
0.8km

Howard

Mammoth Hot Springs

MAMMOTH-NORRIS ROAD

Narrow Gauge Terrace

To Golden Gate

one-way

UPPER TERRACE DRIVE

Canary Spring

MAMMOTH-NORRIS ROAD

one-way

To Norris

↑ **NORTH**

Contour interval 40 feet
Map legend appears on page 6

Narrow Gauge Terrace

Yellowstone was established as the world's first national park, primarily due to its many geothermal features. The Mammoth Hot Springs are some of the most intricate and beautiful of these. If you like to experience thermal features away from boardwalks and crowds, this could be the trail for you. Take this short walk through the forest to one of Yellowstone's most intriguing travertine terraces. *See Plate 1.*

Level of difficulty: Easy

Distance: 1 mile round trip (1.6 km)

Elevation change: A gain of 320 feet in 0.5 mile

Duration: 45 minutes - 1 hour

Best time of year: May through June and September through mid-October (or during the cooler morning and evening hours of summer). This hike is an especially good choice in spring when the higher elevations in the park are still snow-covered.

Trailhead: This hike begins at the Sepulcher/Beaver Ponds Trailhead, located just north of the Mammoth Terraces, between the Liberty Cap rock formation and the stone house, by the parking area designated for buses.

Hiking directions: The trail begins between Clematis Creek and the stone house. It follows the creek for 0.2 mile until it meets the junction with the Howard Eaton Trail. Turn left at this junction. The trail climbs gradually through forest and sagebrush to Narrow Gauge Terrace. Return to the trailhead via the same route. Or, if you'd like to make a loop of this hike, continue along the trail several hundred yards to the Upper Terrace Drive. Turn left on the road and follow it to the boardwalk, which leads back to the parking lot near the trailhead.

Special attention: Thermal features, particularly these hot springs, change frequently. Inquire at the Albright Visitor Center about the current activity in the Narrow Gauge area. Stay on the trail in the thermal area.

Naturalist notes: The stone residence near the trailhead houses the federal magistrate who has jurisdiction in Yellowstone. On the left, you'll pass Hymen Terrace. In the late 1800s, people flocked to natural hot springs all over the country because they believed these waters had medicinal powers. Yellowstone was no exception. For a number of years, the water from this terrace and others was piped into bath houses in the area. This practice was eventually prohibited since it was causing damage to the features and was not in keeping with the park's mission to preserve natural resources for future generations.

On the way up the trail, you'll have good views of Palette Spring and some of the other features. Many visitors notice the large dormant terraces and wonder if these magnificent springs are drying up. Change occurs more rapidly and frequently here than in any of the other hot spring basins in the park. Park rangers notice changes from day to day. The amount of water in the hot spring system is believed to remain constant. So if one spring goes dormant, its water may remain underground or, somewhere else, a new spring may burst to life.

Follow Clematis Creek, which is named for the flowering vine that grows in the area, up the small canyon shaded with Douglas-firs. Soon, you'll come to the junction with the Howard Eaton Trail. Take this trail to the left on its gradual uphill climb through a forest of Douglas-fir and Rocky Mountain juniper and an open area covered with sagebrush. Parts of the original road into the park can be seen from this trail, so you'll be following in the footsteps, or wagon wheel ruts, of early visitors who traveled this way by stagecoach. The trail was named for Howard Eaton, an outfitter who guided visitors around the park on horseback in the early days. The path he followed was a 150-mile loop that roughly parallels the present Grand Loop Road. Some parts of Eaton's route, including this one, are still used as hiking trails.

Around a bend in the trail, Narrow Gauge Terrace will suddenly appear on your left. Though it's uncertain who named this feature, a well known tour guide at the turn of the century, G. L. Henderson, called this long narrow mound the Narrow Gauge because it resembled "a graded road bed ready for tie and rail." It appears that this terrace hasn't changed much from its railroad-like appearance since that time. What has changed is what lies below it.

Continuing down a small spur trail, you'll encounter an interesting array of features. The first springs on this hillside trickled onto the landscape in January of 1978. Terraces are ephemeral, and these have undergone periods of dormancy and activity throughout the years. While enjoying their beauty, you might wonder what nature did to sculpt these fanciful fountains.

Great quantities of rain and snow fall in Yellowstone. This water percolates down into the ground where it's superheated by the heat radiating from partially molten rock a few miles within the earth's crust. This hot water then rises to the surface through cracks in the ground. What makes the Mammoth Hot Springs different from all the other colorful pools in the park is that these hot waters are coming up through limestone rather than the rhyolitic lava that covers much of the park. The results are strikingly different. These springs look like a cave that's been turned inside out, with its delicate formations exposed for all to see.

On the way up through the earth, the water absorbs gasses rising from the magma chamber below, primarily carbon dioxide. The combination of this gas and water creates a weak acid that dissolves the limestone. When exposed to air at the earth's surface, some of the carbon dioxide escapes from this solution. Then, the limestone can no longer remain in solution and it reforms as a solid rock, called travertine. Here, you see new rock being formed before your very eyes. While many geological processes occur over decades and centuries, travertine is created by the minute, by some estimates, as much as 22 inches per year!

Travertine is a white rock, but the terraces are a tapestry of color. Their color is a function of what grows in them. Each color is a type of bacteria adapted to survive in a specific range of high temperatures. You can determine how hot the water is by observing what color bacteria live in it. White and yellow bacteria thrive in water measuring about 167 degrees Fahrenheit. As the water cools, you'll find darker colors like orange, brown, and green.

Science aside, stand back and admire these remarkable creations of nature. An early visitor to the park, Georgina Synge, wrote of them:

At first sight, they look like lovely marble terraces, one above the other. But on approaching them, one discovers that they are little basins of hot water, each delicately ornamented. No human architect ever designed such intricate fountains as these. The water trickles over the edges from one to another, blending them together with the effect of a frozen waterfall.

If you'd like to make a loop of this hike, follow the main trail several hundred yards beyond Narrow Gauge Terrace until it meets the Upper Terrace Drive. Watching for traffic, turn left and walk along the road to the boardwalk trail through the Mammoth Hot Springs. Pick up an area guide from the brochure box in the overlook parking lot and enjoy a leisurely stroll through the terraces.

Whichever way you return, enjoy the fine views of the Mammoth Hot Springs, Fort Yellowstone, and Mount Everts in the distance.

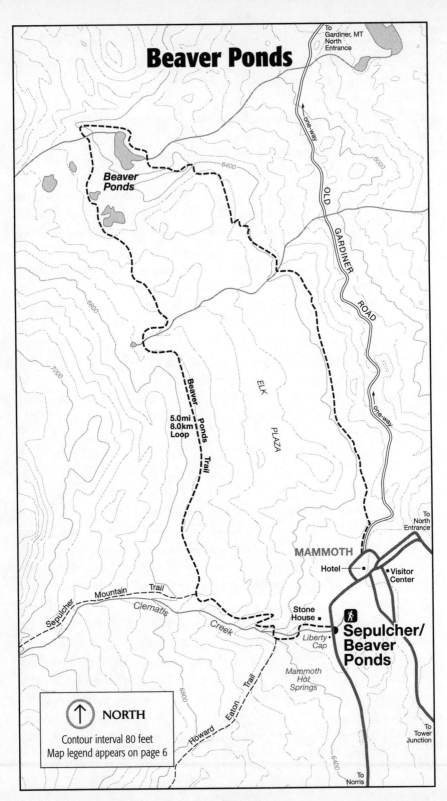

Beaver Ponds

To Gardiner, MT
North Entrance

one-way

OLD GARDINER ROAD

6400

6000

Beaver Ponds

6400

6800

7200

Beaver Ponds Trail

5.0mi
8.0km
Loop

ELK PLAZA

one-way

To North Entrance

MAMMOTH

Hotel

Visitor Center

Mountain Trail

Sepulcher

Clematis

Creek

Stone House

Liberty Cap

Sepulcher/ Beaver Ponds

Mammoth Hot Springs

6800

Eaton Trail

Howard

6400

To Tower Junction

↑ NORTH

Contour interval 80 feet
Map legend appears on page 6

To Norris

...beaver meadows are outspread with charming effect along the banks of the streams.

—Naturalist John Muir, 1885

2

Beaver Ponds

This delightful loop trail takes you to a series of active beaver ponds. Along the way, you travel through a diverse landscape with many moods—from Douglas-fir and aspen groves, and grassy meadows with wildflowers, to open sagebrush plateaus with panoramic views. Because of the diverse habitats, the Beaver Ponds Trail offers good wildlife viewing opportunities, particularly in spring and fall. Mule deer, pronghorn, moose, elk, and black bear, all make this part of the park home as does, of course, the elusive beaver. *See Plate 2.*

Level of difficulty: Moderate

Distance: 5-mile loop (8 km)

Elevation change: A gain of 400 feet in 0.5 mile

Duration: 2 - 4 hours

Best time of year: May through June and September through mid-October (or during the cooler morning and evening hours of summer). The springtime months are optimal for wildflowers. This hike is an especially good choice in spring when the higher elevations in the park are still snow-covered and in the fall when the aspen leaves are changing color.

Trailhead: This hike begins at the Sepulcher/Beaver Ponds Trailhead, located just north of the Mammoth Terraces, between the Liberty Cap rock formation and the stone house, by the parking area designated for buses. Parking is available on the east side of the road.

Hiking directions: The trail starts between the Liberty Cap rock formation and the stone house. It follows the creek up Clematis Gulch for 0.2 mile until it meets the junction with the Howard Eaton Trail. Veer right at this junction, crossing Clematis Creek on a footbridge. The trail climbs about 400 feet in 0.5 mile to the junction with Sepulcher Mountain Trail on the left. Continue straight, through forests and grassy meadows, until you reach the beaver ponds. The trail winds around the ponds and eventually emerges onto a broad sagebrush plateau before it returns to Mammoth Hot Springs.

Special attention: Although this is a loop trail, the hike ends at the entrance to the Old Gardiner Road behind the Mammoth Hotel, a short distance from where you started. To return to the trailhead, walk through the village to the parking area near Liberty Cap.

Naturalist notes: From the trailhead located next to the sandstone residence at the foot of the terraces, follow Clematis Creek upstream. Along the way, you'll enjoy great views of the ephemeral features of Mammoth Hot Springs dominated by Liberty Cap, a massive hot spring cone. In a few hundred yards, the trail crosses the creek and begins a gradual climb through Clematis Gulch. Almost immediately, your surroundings change as you depart the otherworldly feel of the Mammoth Hot Springs for the cool shelter of a Douglas-fir forest. In about 0.2 mile, you'll arrive at the junction with the Howard Eaton Trail, on the left. Head right, crossing Clematis Creek on a footbridge. The trail begins to climb alongside this lively creek through a lush understory of flowers and grasses growing beneath shady stands of large Douglas-firs.

In time, the trail begins to switchback away from the creek, climbing through more open and dry terrain. The Beaver Ponds Trail passes over well-drained glacial soils that receive less snowfall than the higher elevations typical of much of the park. Plants that tolerate such conditions do well here. Among the fir are Rocky Mountain juniper and limber pine, which thrive at lower elevations under dry conditions. In early summer, look for arrowleaf balsamroot adorning the hillsides here in great numbers. Growing in clumps, they favor dry and sunny sites. Their showy yellow flowers add a splash of color to the landscape.

About 0.7 mile from the trailhead, you'll meet the junction for the Sepulcher Mountain Trail. Stay to your right and continue through an open area, where you'll get a good view of some of the terraces of Mammoth Hot Springs in the distance. From here, the trail begins to level off as it leads to the beaver ponds. Enjoy the variety the trail offers as you pass through open stands of young Douglas-fir, occasional wet meadows, beautiful groves of white-barked aspen, and sagebrush covered grasslands. With so many different habitats, the Beaver Ponds Trail is a good place to look for animals. You may see mule deer and elk in the grassy meadows at the edge of the forest, pronghorn among the open sagebrush, and moose in the wet areas around the ponds. Black bears, too, are occasionally found in the forest, so be alert and make noise. The cooler months of spring and fall and the hours of dawn and dusk are the optimum times for observing wildlife. A little later, Fort Yellowstone will come into view on the right.

Sprinkled amid these open forests and grasslands in May and June are wonderful displays of wildflowers. Come fall, the color is overhead, as the aspen leaves begin to turn. On a crisp autumn day against a blue sky, there's nothing quite like the bright yellow glow of the aspen shimmering in the sunshine.

Soon, you'll pass through a dark and moody stand of Douglas-fir near a spring-fed creek. Crossing the stream on a footbridge, you'll arrive at a clearing, greeted by a jubilant grove of aspen. Such are the many moods this trail affords. Before long, you're back among the fir. Ahead, as you descend a small hill, something new lies ahead. Through the trees you can see the first beaver pond.

The trail descends to a large shallow pond lined with reeds and cattails and filled with ducks and other water birds. The throaty call of the yellow-headed blackbird is distinctive, as is its black and yellow plumage. Perhaps naturalist John Muir captured the scene best on his 1885 visit to the park: ...*beaver meadows are outspread with charming effect along the banks of the streams, parklike expanses in the woods, and innumerable small gardens in rocky recesses of the mountains,...while the whole wilderness is enlivened with happy animals.*

The trail continues to wind past several ponds of various sizes and depths, on footbridges over small streams and wetlands. After crossing a swiftly flowing stream, the trail turns sharply right and begins to follow the water as it tumbles downstream. Here's where the beaver enters the picture. With its huge chisel-like incisors, this animal is made for cutting wood. Imagine this industrious, bucktoothed creature engineering a dam across this stream, using only the materials at hand: the wood from these aspen and fir forests. By impounding the water, it creates a different habitat, which benefits other creatures who take advantage of his creation.

The largest pond lies below this little stream; the trail skirts its edge. Look closely and you'll see a lodge built on the opposite bank and a dam near the end of the pond. A dam is an interwoven network of branches and sticks plastered together with mud. A beaver's dam can be quite the architectural wonder; some in Yellowstone stand 6 to 8 feet high and stretch as much as a quarter mile long. If you hope to see these engineers of nature, your best opportunity is just before sunset when they are more active. Daytime sightings are rare.

Historically, the story of the beaver is the saga of the exploration of the continent. In the early 1800s, fur trappers delved deeply into the wild recesses of North America in search of the beaver's pelt. Their exploits helped open the continent to settlement, but resulted in the extinction of this large rodent from many locales. Conservation measures have since helped restore this creature to its rightful place as the chief architect of the animal kingdom.

As you continue around this beaver pond, you'll cross the outlet creek. From here, the trail travels another two miles through more Douglas-fir and aspen before opening up onto a broad sagebrush plateau known as Elk Plaza. Look for the distinctively marked pronghorn, who favors the grasses and sagebrush found here. This fleet-footed creature can reach speeds of seventy miles per hour, making it the fastest land animal in North America. In this open country, you'll be afforded sweeping views of northern Yellowstone. In the distance, you can see the small north entrance town of Gardiner, Montana, with the Absaroka Mountains towering above. To your right (west) is Sepulcher Mountain and on the left is the long ridge of Mount Everts. To your left, you'll see the Gardner River below and Bunsen Peak looming ahead.

Eventually, the trail parallels the Old Gardiner Road to the left. This 1880s stagecoach route is now a 5-mile, one-way drive from Mammoth to the North Entrance. As you come to the trail's end, the Mammoth Hot Springs reappear. Imagine being one of the first explorers to gaze upon this fantastic scene. What words come to mind to describe such a sight? As you look down on Mammoth village, you can also see the red-roofed buildings of historic Fort Yellowstone. Built from 1891 to 1913, Fort Yellowstone was home to the U.S. Cavalry, which protected Yellowstone for 32 years prior to the establishment of the National Park Service. Today, it serves as park headquarters. A self-guiding tour of the fort departs from the front of the visitor center.

The Beaver Ponds Trail ends back in Mammoth village at the beginning of the Old Gardiner Road behind the hotel. From here, it's a short walk back to the trailhead near Liberty Cap.

We beheld the far-famed Hoodoo Rocks—a wrecked
mountain where giants once played.
—Park visitor Joe Mitchell Chapple, 1922

The Hoodoos &
Snow Pass/Hoodoos Loop

This trail displays a tremendous array of mountain scenery. In a sweeping loop around Terrace Mountain, you'll see fine views of one of Yellowstone's highest peaks, you'll walk through the forested canyon of Snow Pass, and you'll experience the otherworldly rock formations known as "the Hoodoos." A shorter, more direct route to the Hoodoos is an option, if you have limited time. *See Plate 3.*

The Hoodoos

Level of difficulty: Moderate

Distance: 3 miles round trip (4.8 km)

Elevation change: A gain of 250 feet in 1 mile

Duration: 1 - 2 hours

Snow Pass/Hoodoos Loop

Level of difficulty: Moderate

Distance: 6.2 miles round trip (10 km)

Elevation change: A total gain of 640 feet

Duration: 3 - 4 hours

Best time of year: Mid-May through early July and September through October (or during the cooler morning and evening hours of summer). Snow may persist on Snow Pass in May. The springtime months are optimal for wildflowers.
Trailhead: This hike begins at the Glen Creek Trailhead, which is a pullout on the east side of the road, 5 miles (8 km) south of Mammoth Hot Springs on the Mammoth/Norris Road. This is also the trailhead for the Bunsen Peak Trail.

Hiking directions: From the parking area, carefully cross the road and begin on the trail on the south side of Glen Creek. In 0.2 mile, you'll reach a large trail-

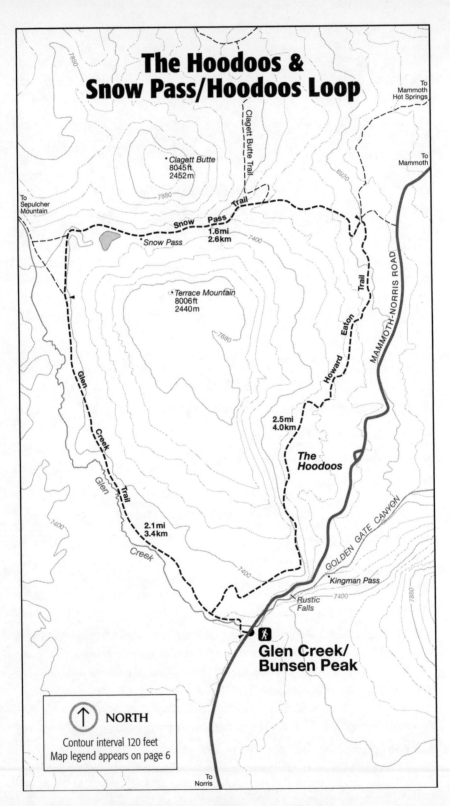

The Hoodoos &
Snow Pass/Hoodoos Loop

Clagett Butte
8045ft
2452m

Clagett Butte Trail

To
Mammoth
Hot Springs

To
Mammoth

To
Sepulcher
Mountain

Snow Pass Trail

Snow Pass

1.6mi
2.6km

Terrace Mountain
8006ft
2440m

Howard Eaton Trail

MAMMOTH-NORRIS ROAD

2.5mi
4.0km

The Hoodoos

Glen Creek Trail

2.1mi
3.4km

Creek

GOLDEN GATE CANYON

Kingman Pass

Rustic
Falls

Glen Creek/
Bunsen Peak

NORTH

Contour interval 120 feet
Map legend appears on page 6

To
Norris

24

head bulletin board. Here, you'll find the junction with the Howard Eaton Trail, which heads into the woods to the right. This is the direct route to the Hoodoos. It climbs a steep hill and then descends into the Hoodoos. Return to the trailhead by the same route.

If you're taking the Snow Pass/Hoodoos Loop Trail, bypass this junction and proceed straight along Glen Creek for 2.1 miles to the Snow Pass Trail. Veer right at the unsigned "Y" junction and continue over Snow Pass for 1.2 miles, where you'll meet the Clagett Butte Trail. Continue straight and descend 0.4 mile to the Howard Eaton Trail. Turn right and follow the Howard Eaton Trail as it climbs steadily up to the Hoodoos. Beyond the Hoodoos, the trail ascends along a steep hillside before it rejoins the Glen Creek Trail at the trailhead bulletin board. Turn left, cross the road, and return to the parking area.

Special attention: Both grizzly and black bears have been known to use this trail. Be alert and make noise before blind curves or hills, when you can't see clearly in all directions.

Naturalist notes: If you're going directly to the Hoodoos, turn right on the Howard Eaton Trail, which begins several hundred yards up the Glen Creek Trail. You can drive through a small area of hoodoos just south of Mammoth Hot Springs, but not acres of them as you'll find here. Climbing 250 feet along the side of a steep hill, you'll reach these jumbled blocks of travertine in one mile. The explanation of these intriguing rock formations can be found in the last three paragraphs of the Naturalist Notes. Return to the trailhead by the same route.

If you're hiking the Snow Pass/Hoodoos Loop, the trail follows Glen Creek as it meanders through the sagebrush at the edge of the forest. On your way up this open valley, look for coyotes slipping stealthily through the brush. Sandhill cranes may also be seen here, although their light brown color camouflages them well.

This leg of the trail is distinguished by the views of the impressive mountain peaks that surround it. To the right is Terrace Mountain. In the course of the hike, you'll be circling this unusual mountain made of dormant hot spring terraces. To the left are the peaks of the Gallatin Range, most notably Mount Holmes, Dome Mountain, Antler Peak and Quadrant Mountain. The summit that dominates the skyline, however, is Electric Peak, straight ahead.

At 10,992 feet, Electric is the highest peak in the Gallatin Range and the sixth highest in the park. Electric Peak began to form as sediments were laid down in an ancient sea. About 50 million years ago, it was covered by lava and was later sculpted by glaciers during the most recent ice age. This striking mountain was named because Henry Gannet, a member of the Hayden Survey of 1872, was nearly struck by lightning on its summit. Gannet was taking measurements on the peak when an electrical current began to pass through his body. His colleagues recall watching him run down the mountain, surrounded by a loud electrical crackling noise, with his hair standing on end. Gannet survived the incident and earned the right to name this peak. His experience reminds us all to beware of thunderstorms on exposed mountaintops.

In 2.1 miles, you'll reach an unmarked fork in the trail. At this "Y" junction, take the trail to the right as it begins to wind around Terrace Mountain. You'll be following power lines for a short while, but this intrusion won't last long. Passing through a boggy wetland, you begin your gradual ascent to Snow Pass. Here, the canyon narrows between the walls of Terrace Mountain and Clagett Butte. The changing forest varies between lodgepole pine, limber pine, spruce, fir, and aspen. Before long, you reach the top of the pass. Even at 7,400 feet, this is probably among the least strenuous mountain passes you'll ever experience. Still, celebrate your accomplishment by enjoying the distant view of Mount Everts to the northeast.

Soon, you'll pass the junction with the Clagett Butte Trail. This large butte was named by the first Park Service Superintendent of Yellowstone, Horace Albright, to honor William Horace Clagett, the congressional representative from the Montana Territory who introduced the bill that would establish Yellowstone as a national park.

Once past this junction, the trail begins to descend to the right around Terrace Mountain. Had you hiked up Snow Pass from the other direction, you wouldn't have found it so pleasantly gradual. Part of this route over Snow Pass was the original stagecoach road that brought visitors into the park from Mammoth Hot Springs. Early visitors complained bitterly about "this terrible hill" which, at the time, was believed to be the only passable route to the rest of the park. The heavy snow that gave this pass its name was known to block this section of road, sometimes until late summer. A senator from New York, Roscoe Conkling, visiting in 1883, was so frightened by this pass that he curtailed his visit to Yellowstone at this point and returned home. That year, Army Corps Engineer Dan Kingman began work on the new road around the rock cliffs known as the Golden Gate Canyon.

As you descend this hill, you'll see sections of the old stagecoach road, but you probably won't find it so terrible. The lush growth of vegetation here includes low-lying Rocky Mountain juniper as well as buffaloberries that attract black bears here in mid- to late summer. Make noise when hiking this part of the trail!

At the bottom of the hill, a large bulletin board marks the junction with the Howard Eaton Trail. Turn right here. You'll immediately notice a few large trees that have been snapped off at their bases, perhaps by powerful winds. This is a fitting gateway to the eerie world of the Hoodoos you'll enter on this leg of the journey. But before you get there, the trail winds and climbs through an aspen grove and open forests with striking views of Mount Everts, Bunsen Peak, and the Washburn Range in the distance. The trail continues to steepen until it reaches the Hoodoos.

In the Hoodoos, you may feel as if you're on a different planet. These oddly shaped rocks are not really "hoodoos." Hoodoo is actually a technical term for a different type of formation found predominantly in the southwestern parks. This name was given to these rocks, not because of their geological origin, but because of their ghostly appearance. Even today, this vast area has a surreal feel to it, particularly after the searing effects of the fires in 1988. Park visitor Joe Mitchell Chapple wrote of them in 1922: *Riding along the rocky ledge, we beheld the far-famed Hoodoo Rocks, lying together in massed confusion, rectangular in form—a wrecked mountain where giants once played.*

It may be hard to imagine that Terrace Mountain, which looms before you, was once an exquisitely beautiful travertine terrace much like the Mammoth Hot Springs are today. 65,000 years ago, the springs on this mountain were active. Thousands of years ago, they became dormant as these features are known to do. A combination of glaciers and earthquakes pulled the blocks of travertine down the hill, leaving the jumbled pile of rocks before you.

Leaving this enchanted world, the trail climbs out of the Hoodoos. It clings to a steep hillside, in and out of the forest, sometimes in view of the road. When you reach the yellowish cliffs, you'll be walking through the rock that comprises Golden Gate Canyon. This rock formation resulted from a volcanic eruption about two million years ago. The explosive force of the volcanic gasses shattered the molten magma into millions of particles of ash. This cloud of ash was so hot that when it settled, it solidified into rock. The resulting rock, known as welded tuff, is pale in color. This, combined with the orange lichens that grow on the rocks, give this gateway its golden cast. You'll also get a sense for the engineering wonder that Lt. Kingman orchestrated to build a road along this wall of rock. This section of road still bears his name today, Kingman Pass.

From a high point on the trail, you'll be treated to fine views of Rustic Falls (which is Glen Creek dropping 47 feet), Swan Lake, and the peaks of the Gallatin Range. You've come full circle. The trail then descends through the forest to the junction with the Glen Creek Trailhead. Turn left here and return to the parking area. Your adventure in this unusual world is complete!

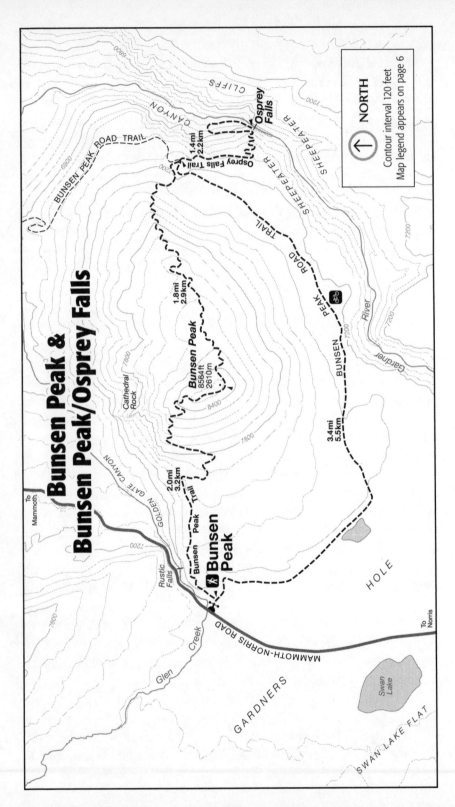

Bunsen Peak &
Bunsen Peak/Osprey Falls

NORTH

Contour interval 120 feet
Map legend appears on page 6

Osprey Falls

BUNSEN PEAK ROAD TRAIL

Osprey Falls Trail

1.4mi
2.2km

CANYON

CLIFFS

SHEEPEATER

ROAD TRAIL

BUNSEN PEAK

1.8mi
2.9km

Bunsen Peak
8564ft
2610m

Cathedral
Rock

Gardner River

3.4mi
5.5km

2.0mi
3.2km

Bunsen Peak Trail

GOLDEN GATE CANYON

To Mammoth

Rustic Falls

Glen Creek

Bunsen Peak

MAMMOTH-NORRIS ROAD

To Norris

GARDNERS HOLE

Swan Lake

SWAN LAKE FLAT

28

...take a look into a few of the...volumes of the grand geological library of the park and see how God writes history. No technical knowledge is required; only a calm day and a calm mind.

—Naturalist John Muir, 1885

4

Bunsen Peak & Bunsen Peak/Osprey Falls

Here's a hike that covers a lot of ground, from mountaintop to canyon bottom. First, scale the heights of Bunsen Peak, the remains of an ancient volcano, for wonderful views of northern Yellowstone, including Gardners Hole, Mammoth Hot Springs, Electric Peak, and the Gallatin Range. If you're feeling a bit more ambitious, venture down the mountain into the depths of magnificent Sheepeater Canyon, home to one of Yellowstone's little-seen treasures, beautiful 150-foot Osprey Falls. The hikes to Bunsen Peak and Osprey Falls can be done individually or as a combination. *See Plate 4.*

Bunsen Peak

Level of difficulty: Strenuous

Distance: 4 miles round trip (6.4 km)

Elevation change: A gain of 1,300 feet in 2 miles

Duration: 2 - 3 hours

Bunsen Peak/Osprey Falls

Level of difficulty: Strenuous

Distance: 10-mile loop (16 km)

Elevation change: A gain of 1,300 feet in 2 miles, then a loss of 800 feet in 1.0 mile and subsequent climb up

Duration: 6 - 8 hours

Best time of year: June through early July and September through October (or during the cooler morning and evening hours of summer). Snow may persist on Bunsen Peak through May.

Trailhead: This hike begins from the parking area for the Bunsen Peak Trailhead on the east side of the road, 5 miles (8 km) south of Mammoth Hot Springs on the Mammoth-Norris Road.

Hiking directions: From the parking area, walk past the barricade of the old Bunsen Peak Road to where the trail begins on the left. Hike the 2-mile trail as it switchbacks 1,300 feet up to the top of Bunsen Peak. If this is your final destination, return to the trailhead by the same route.

For those doing the 10-mile loop to Osprey Falls, continue past the summit following the trail down the east side of the mountain to where it meets the Bunsen Peak Road again. Turn left on the road. Soon, on your right, you'll meet the trail to Osprey Falls. Hike 1.4 miles down Sheepeater Canyon to a view of the falls. From here, it's an 800-foot climb out of the canyon and back to the road, where you'll turn left and continue 3.4 miles back to the trailhead.

If you wish to go only to Osprey Falls, you can hike or bike the Bunsen Peak Road 3.4 miles to where it meets the trail to the falls. From here, hike the 2.8 miles down to the falls and back, before returning to the trailhead via the old road. The total distance is 9.6 miles. This alternative is a good option for mountain bikers. However, for hikers we recommend the loop trail that includes Bunsen Peak, which is only 0.4 mile longer, albeit 1,300 feet more in elevation gain. The views are worth it!

Special attention: Keep a safe distance from the telecommunications equipment the National Park Service maintains on the summit of Bunsen Peak. The trail down Sheepeater Canyon to Osprey Falls is steep. Wear good hiking boots for traction and watch your footing on loose rocks.

Naturalist notes: Bunsen Peak is a relic of geologic time. Many geologists believe it is the eroding remains of an ancient volcanic cone that formed some 50 million years ago. Today, what's left is an 8,564-foot peak, offering those who hike it an impressive view of the surrounding scenery and geology of northern Yellowstone. You'll be rewarded with great views for your efforts.

Bunsen Peak was named by members of the Hayden Geological Survey in 1872 in recognition of the work of noted German physicist Robert Wilhelm Bunsen. Bunsen never visited Yellowstone, but his studies of the geysers of Iceland and the theories he developed as to how they work prompted the Geological Survey to acknowledge his contributions by naming this mountain in his honor. Today, though his theories on geysers are forgotten, he is remembered for inventing the laboratory instrument known as the Bunsen burner.

The trail begins its gradual climb above the narrow canyon of Golden Gate, through which the road passes on the left. One of the original stagecoach roads through Yellowstone passed through this small opening in the rock, making this the "gateway" to the rest of the park. The Golden Gate Canyon is composed of volcanic rock a mere 2 million years old, compared to the much older Bunsen Peak rocks ahead. This more recent eruption spewed large quantities of hot volcanic ash into the air. As the ash settled and cooled, it formed a solid rock known as welded tuff.

The geologic story of Bunsen Peak is a little less clear. Bunsen consists of dacite, a volcanic rock that cooled within the earth before being exposed at the surface. Many geologists believe that this peak formed about 50 million years ago as part of the massive volcanic period that created the Absaroka Range. The lava that surrounds it has eroded away, leaving only the core of the old volcano.

Above Golden Gate, the trail levels off through a forest of burned lodgepole pine and Douglas-fir. In this land born of fire, here is a mountain that has been touched by fire many times. Wildfires burned the slopes of Bunsen Peak in 1886 and again in 1988. These fires have produced forests of varying ages, demonstrating the beneficial role natural fire plays in diversifying a landscape. Notice the classic mosaic pattern of burned and unburned trees fashioned by the great fires of 1988. Such a patchwork benefits grazing wildlife who prefer the new "edges" of habitat the fires created.

Soon, the trail bends to the right and enters an open grassy area with few trees. To the south and west, you see the expansive valley of Gardners Hole and Swan Lake framed by the southern extent of the impressive Gallatin Range. At 10,992 feet, Electric Peak, the most prominent mountain in the Gallatins, towers in the distance beyond Terrace Mountain. The valley before you is home to a variety of wildlife. Elk, bison, and mule deer are often seen here, as is the occasional pronghorn, coyote, or black bear. In Swan Lake Flat, sandhill cranes are frequently spotted along with numerous ducks on the lake. The rare trumpeter swan has also been known to grace this lake that bears its name.

The origins of this valley are linked to the mountains that bound it to the west. Many of the powerful forces of nature joined together to create the Gallatin Range. The base of these mountains is composed of some of the oldest rock on earth from the "basement" of geologic time. 100 million years ago, they were covered by a vast inland sea. The sand, sediments, and marine life within these waters were compressed to form sandstone, shale, and limestone. Later, the earth rose along a major fault and tilted to the north, lifting the mountains on one side, as the other side dropped to form the broad valleys of Swan Lake Flat and Gardners Hole. The finishing touches were added by glaciers that scoured the valley floor and sculpted the peaks you see today.

The trail begins to gain more elevation as it turns back to the left and travels the length of a long switchback. Here is a wonderful view of majestic Cathedral Rock, jutting out of the northern slopes of Bunsen Peak.

The terraces of Mammoth Hot Springs stand out prominently, as do the nearby red-roofed buildings of the park's headquarters, the historic Fort

Yellowstone. The long ridge of Mount Everts stands beyond them. The bright colored rock atop this plateau is more of the volcanic welded tuff you encountered earlier at Golden Gate. Closer to you are the Hoodoos, the jumbled blocks of travertine that fell from Terrace Mountain, where hot springs once flowed thousands of years ago.

Then, the trail steepens, passing over talus slopes amid a Douglas-fir forest as it climbs a series of short switchbacks in the final 0.5 mile to the rocky summit. Once you're on top of Bunsen Peak, a host of mountain ranges surround you: the Washburn Range to the east and the Red Mountains far to the south. On clear days, even the Grand Tetons can be seen rising above the horizon, well over 60 miles away. In 1885, amid this magnificent mountain scenery, naturalist John Muir implored: ...*take a look into a few of the...volumes of the grand geological library of the park and see how God writes history. No technical knowledge is required; only a calm day and a calm mind.*

Use caution while passing the telecommunications towers and equipment. If the summit of Bunsen Peak was your destination for the day, return to the trailhead by the same route.

For those heading on to Osprey Falls, continue hiking beyond the summit. The trail winds down the east slope of Bunsen Peak to the Bunsen Peak Road. On the way down, the route switchbacks away from the views just described, traveling through a largely burned forest of Douglas-fir. As you reach the bottom of the hill, the old road comes into view. The trail you're on parallels this road. To reach the Osprey Falls trailhead, however, take the spur trail that turns sharply left at a large partially burned tree in the open meadow. This path winds back for a short while before crossing the road to the trailhead.

The distance to Osprey Falls is 1.4 miles. The trail begins by paralleling the rim of Sheepeater Canyon. The park's second superintendent, Philetus Norris, named the southern walls of the canyon opposite you "Sheepeater Cliffs" in honor of the only Native Americans believed to reside in Yellowstone year round. Exploring this deep chasm in 1879, Norris discovered a recently deserted site where a group of Sheepeater Indians had been living.

Having never adopted the horse, the Tukudeka, or Sheepeater, lived in the mountains of Yellowstone where they hunted bighorn sheep, elk, and deer. They were renowned for their prized bows, which they fashioned from the ram's horn of the mountain sheep. Fur trapper Osborne Russell described his friendly encounters with the Tukudeka during his travels through Yellowstone in the 1830s:

They were all neatly clothed in...Sheep skins of the best quality and seemed to be perfectly contented and happy...They were well armed with bows and arrows pointed with obsidian. The bows were beautifully wrought from the Sheep, Buffaloe, and Elk horns, secured with Deer and Elk sinews and ornamented with porcupine quills...We obtained a large number of Elk, Deer, and Sheep skins from them of the finest quality and three large neatly dressed Panther Skins...They would throw the skins at our feet and say "give us whatever you please for them and we are satisfied. We can get plenty of Skins but we do not often see the Tibuboes (or People of the Sun)."

In addition to their prowess as bow hunters, there's evidence that the Tukudeka also herded the bighorn sheep off steep cliffs. Norris found chutes constructed of lodgepole pines at the top of Rustic Falls, through which the Tukudeka drove the animals over the falls into the narrow gorge of the Golden Gate Canyon. Although there's no proof, Sheepeater Cliffs could also have been used in this manner. Look for the bighorn among these precipitous walls across the canyon. Their presence here today continues to evoke the memory of the native people who once dwelled in these mountains.

After following the rim for about 0.4 mile, the trail enters Sheepeater Canyon for the 1-mile, 800-foot descent to Osprey Falls. Distinguished by the distinctive columns of basalt composing its walls, this deep canyon is one of the most impressive gorges you'll see anywhere in the park. Be careful of loose rocks on the steep switchbacks.

Greeting you below is the powerful Gardner River, which carved this impressive canyon. The roar of the river grows louder as it tumbles over the rocks in its path. With such a river beside you, racing with terrific force, you can imagine the magnitude of the falls that await you. The air grows cooler and the torrent increases as you crest a small hill and Osprey Falls comes suddenly into view. Tucked in this dark narrow canyon, the Gardner River plunges 150 feet over a steep ledge as Osprey Falls, and then, without hesitation, rushes onward. The trail ends at the foot of the falls, where its waters pound the rock and send a fine mist through the air. Linger near the edge of Osprey Falls as long as time will permit. Drink in this splendid spot, seen by relatively few park visitors each year.

When the time comes to depart, make the long climb out of Sheepeater Canyon and back to the Bunsen Peak Road. At the road, turn left and continue 3.4 miles back to the trailhead. This old roadbed skirts the southern base of Bunsen Peak. Although it passes through a few aspen, Douglas-fir, and lodgepole pine along the way, the road travels through mostly open sagebrush-covered grasslands. This stretch of trail can be particularly good for wildlife viewing during the cool morning and early evening hours, with elk, mule deer, and bison commonly seen grazing nearby. Nearer the trailhead, you'll encouner some wet meadows and ponds that lure both the hiker and a variety of waterfowl.

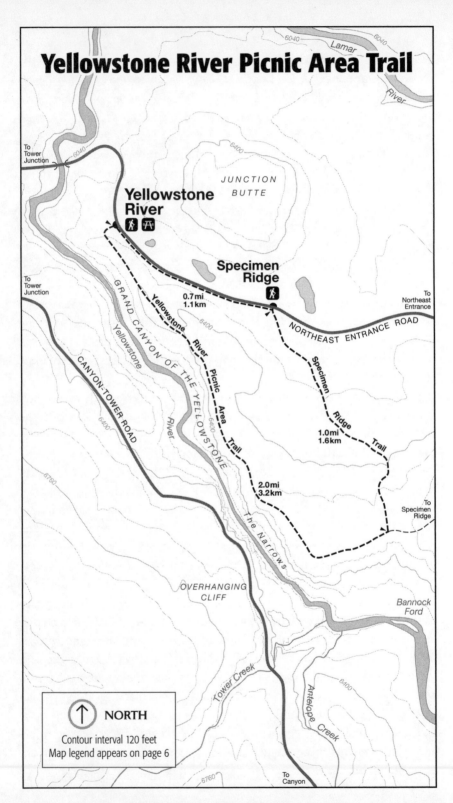

Yellowstone River Picnic Area Trail

6040 Lamar River

To Tower Junction

JUNCTION BUTTE

Yellowstone River

Specimen Ridge

6400

0.7mi
1.1km

To Tower Junction

To Northeast Entrance

NORTHEAST ENTRANCE ROAD

GRAND CANYON OF THE YELLOWSTONE

Yellowstone River

Yellowstone River Picnic Area Trail

Specimen Ridge Trail

1.0mi
1.6km

CANYON-TOWER ROAD

6400

6760

2.0mi
3.2km

To Specimen Ridge

The Narrows

OVERHANGING CLIFF

Bannock Ford

Tower Creek

Antelope Creek

6400

↑ NORTH

Contour interval 120 feet
Map legend appears on page 6

6760

To Canyon

On the Yellowstone [River]...huge basaltic cliffs and columns rose to a height of six hundred feet, looking like castles...

—Explorer Walter Trumball, 1870

The Yellowstone River Picnic Area Trail

This trail follows the rim of the northernmost reaches of the Grand Canyon of the Yellowstone River. A walk along "the Narrows" of this great canyon is a journey during which evidence of epochs of geological time unfolds before you. The trail along the bluff is a leisurely 2-mile stroll. Here, you can decide to either return along the canyon rim or take a loop trail back through grassy meadows to the parking area. The last part of this loop is along the road, but the ponds, marsh, and birdlife make even this leg of the trail enjoyable. *See Plate 5.*

Level of difficulty: Easy

Distance: 3.7-mile loop (5.9 km)

Elevation change: A gain of 200 feet in 0.5 mile

Duration: $1\frac{1}{2}$ - $2\frac{1}{2}$ hours

Best time of year: May through June and September through October (or during the cooler morning and evening hours of summer). The springtime months are optimal for wildflowers.

Trailhead: This hike begins at the Yellowstone River Picnic Area, 1.3 mile (2.1 km) east of Tower Junction on the Northeast Entrance Road.

Hiking directions: The trail starts from the trail sign on the east side of the parking lot. It climbs gradually, 200 feet in elevation, up to the rim of the Canyon, and continues for 1.5 miles to the end of a high bluff. From here, you can either retrace your steps to the trailhead, or make the trail into a loop. To do the latter, continue to the left down the hill to the junction with the Specimen Ridge Trail. Turn left here and follow the trail as it winds through forest and meadow to the Northeast Entrance Road. Turn left on the road and walk 0.7 miles back to the Yellowstone River Picnic Area.

Special attention: Be cautious of steep drop-offs into the canyon below. This is bear country. Be alert and make noise if at any point you can't see clearly in all directions. If you take the loop trail, watch for traffic as you walk along the roadside.

Naturalist notes: Hiking the Yellowstone River Picnic Area Trail is a wonderful way to celebrate spring. The wildflowers are prolific, the views of the snow-capped mountains inspiring, and the encounter with the canyon, grand.

The trail climbs gradually up a grassy sagebrush-covered hillside, skirting a Douglas fir forest. It parallels the road below for a short while, with the flat-topped Junction Butte off to the left rising boldly from the valley floor. Near the ridgetop, the forest changes from lodgepole pine to Douglas-fir. The farther you ascend this small hill, the more spectacular become the views of the mountains in the distance, from the Absarokas to the east to the Washburn Range to the south. Soon, you'll be hiking on a ridge between the Tower and Northeast Entrance roads. But don't let this touch of civilization deter you. The scenery is awesome enough to command your complete attention. Such an intrusion will seem trivial. For this leg of the journey, your eyes will be drawn to the skies, but the sound of the Yellowstone River coming into earshot below is a hint of the geological curiosities that you will soon discover.

The huge boulders strewn erratically along the way are just that—glacial "erratics," rocks that were plucked from the Beartooth Plateau to the east, carried along in a glacier, and then deposited here randomly as the ice melted about 12,000 years ago. You'll notice that some of these large rocks have a single tree growing next to them. These are known as "nurse rocks." The protection of these rocks creates a micro-climate, a shady, moist place for Douglas-fir seedlings to survive in this hot dry setting.

This high plateau with steep cliffs is excellent habitat for the bighorn sheep. You may see them here, and if you do, give them a wide berth. The ability to deftly climb to these precipitous spots is their primary defense from predators.

Soon the Yellowstone River comes into view, intermittently at first, but shortly it will accompany you on your travels along the bluff. The canyon of the Yellowstone River is better known for its storied falls and colorful walls miles upriver. However, the story this stretch of the canyon has to tell is no less fascinating. This more constricted part of the canyon is known as "the Narrows," and it exposes a remarkable slice of geologic time. At a glance, you become witness to millions of years of the power of the earth. At the bottom of the canyon are dark cliffs that were laid down during volcanic events around 50 million years ago and, above them, the lighter gravels left by ancient streams. On top of these are columns of lava from a much younger volcanic episode and, finally, the deposits from the most recent glaciers, on which you're standing today.

The distinctive columns across the river in the massive "Overhanging Cliff" are created when a type of lava called basalt shrinks as it cools, much like cracks form in mud when the water evaporates, leaving interesting geometric shapes.

As if enough geologic wonders haven't been paraded before you, you'll also see tall spires or pinnacles lining the canyon.

This magnificent canyon, with its unusual and sometimes otherworldly rock formations, seemed to capture the imagination of Walter Trumball while on expedition here in 1870. This exploring party was going into somewhat unknown and uncharted lands with some trepidation. These fears came through in their reflections on this unusual part of the canyon.

On the Yellowstone…huge basaltic cliffs and columns rose to a height of six hundred feet,…the rocks were worn into curious and fantastic shapes, looking, in daylight, like spires or steeples, but in the moonlight, reminding one of the portal of an old castle,…[with] a number of the fabled genies standing ready to hurl adventurous mortals into the gorge below, which was enveloped by the shadows of the night in impenetrable darkness.

You won't have to worry about any mortal-hurling genies today. You can just enjoy the extraordinary scenery.

This short trail presents a textbook of geologic features. Take a moment away from your study of rocks, though, to enjoy the wildlife you may see along the way. The cheerful chirp of the yellow-bellied marmot may draw you out of your reverie of ancient geological times. Basking in the sun, these critters encourage us all to relax on these lazy summer days.

As you reach the end of the promontory, this geologic story takes a cultural turn. Below you, both Tower and Antelope creeks join the Yellowstone River. Near the small island where the river turns is the Bannock Ford, the place where the Bannock Indians, among others, forded the Yellowstone River on their way to hunt buffalo.

From this historic point, you have the option of retracing your steps along the rim to the trailhead, or taking a loop trail back. To make a loop of it, walk downhill to the junction with the Specimen Ridge Trail. Turn left here and follow the trail as it winds through meadows with stands of aspen and Douglas-fir. In spring and early summer, a profusion of wildflowers splashes color across this grassland. As you hike gradually downhill, enjoy the mountain scenery. Once at the road, turn left. On this leisurely walk back to the Yellowstone River Picnic Area, you'll pass several marshy areas where you may see yellow-headed blackbirds perched proudly on tall reeds.

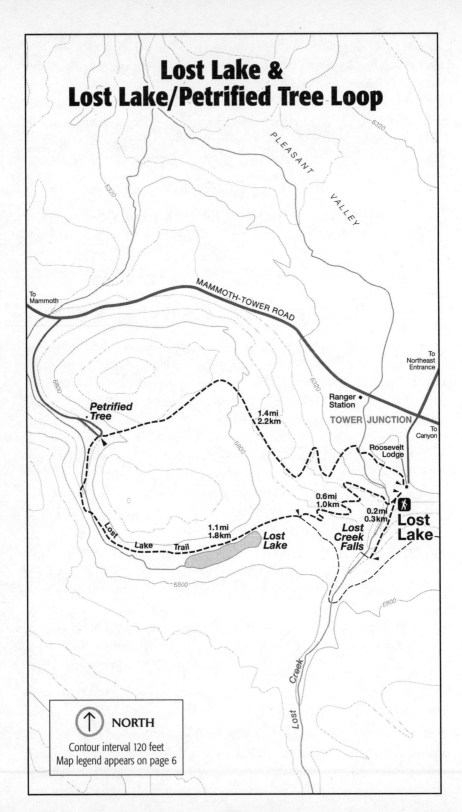

Lost Lake &
Lost Lake/Petrified Tree Loop

PLEASANT VALLEY

6320

6320

MAMMOTH-TOWER ROAD

To Mammoth

6800

6320

Petrified Tree

1.4mi
2.2km

6800

Ranger Station

To Northeast Entrance

TOWER JUNCTION

To Canyon

Roosevelt Lodge

0.6mi
1.0km

0.2mi
0.3km

Lost
Lake
Trail

1.1mi
1.8km

Lost Lake

Lost Creek Falls

Lost Lake

6800

6800

Lost Creek

NORTH

Contour interval 120 feet
Map legend appears on page 6

Lost Creek Falls is well worthy of a visit. The formation of the walls is very unusual, and the water pours over the brink in a light spray which forms...a scene of quiet beauty rarely found in so wild and rough a country.

—Park Guidebook, 1903

6

Lost Lake & Lost Lake/Petrified Tree Loop

This is a delightfully diverse walk to several "lost" places. The Lost Creek Falls hike is one of the shortest walks to a beautiful waterfall in the park. Lost Lake is a lovely place to find yourself. If you'd like a longer walk, a loop trail presents fine views of a petrified tree and the Absaroka and Beartooth mountains. *See Plate 6.*

Lost Lake

Level of difficulty: Moderate

Distance: 2 miles round trip (3.2 km)

Elevation change: A gain of 360 feet in 0.6 mile

Duration: 1 - 2 hours

Lost Lake/Petrifed Tree Loop

Level of difficulty: Moderate

Distance: 3.5-mile loop (5.6 km)

Elevation change: A total gain of 600 feet

Duration: 2 - 3 hours

Best time of year: June through September (during the cooler morning and evening hours).

Trailhead: This hike begins directly behind Roosevelt Lodge, which is located at Tower Junction. As an alternative, this loop trail can also be hiked originating from the Petrified Tree parking area, 1.4 miles (2.6 km) west of Tower Junction.

Hiking directions: From the trailhead register behind Roosevelt Lodge, the trail immediately forks. To go to Lost Creek Falls, take the left fork, which leads gradually uphill for 0.2 mile to the falls. After viewing the falls, retrace your steps to the trailhead. To go to Lost Lake, take the fork to the right, which crosses the creek and winds up 360 feet in 0.6 mile in a series of switchbacks. At the top of the hill, turn right at the trail junction. In 0.2 mile, you'll reach Lost Lake. If you're not making the loop trail via the petrified tree, return to the trailhead by the same route.

If you plan to make the loop to the petrified tree, continue beyond Lost Lake. The trail bends to the right, following a creek through a narrow ravine. The ravine soon opens up at the parking area for the petrified tree. The trail skirts the end of the parking area and veers to the right, climbing 200 feet away from the parking area, up a steep hill. It continues across a sagebrush plateau. Proceed straight until the trail begins to wind down through the forest to the Tower Ranger Station area. Once in the service area behind the ranger station, locate the orange markers across the creek and follow them up to the cabins at Roosevelt Lodge.

Special attention: Black bears are known to frequent this area during the summer months. Be alert and make noise if at any point you can't see clearly in all directions. Also, groups on horseback use this trail regularly. If you encounter such a group, move off to the downhill side of the trail until they pass.

Naturalist notes: Don't miss the remarkable short ramble up to Lost Creek Falls. Take the left fork of the trail and walk along Lost Creek as it cascades joyfully around and over large granite boulders on its way down from the falls. The Douglas-fir trees that fill this narrow canyon provide a pleasant shade over the rocky trail as it ascends gradually for a mere 0.2 mile. Geologist William Holmes named this stream in 1878: *I have called it Lost Creek, because it apparently sinks from sight in the lower part of its course…* The creek is clearly in evidence here as it drops gracefully, 40 feet, to the canyon below. Rock pinnacles line the canyon like the turrets of a castle, guarding the secret of this delightful spot.

Once back at the trailhead, take the right fork to reach Lost Lake. The trail crosses a footbridge over Lost Creek and climbs through a dense forest with a luxuriant understory of thimbleberries, raspberries, and a variety of wildflowers. While resting on the switchbacks, you'll notice that many of the Douglas-fir trees on this hillside have died. They succumbed to an infestation of the western budworm during the 1970s. The stringy black lichen hanging from their branches is known as "old man's beard."

At the top of the hill, turn right at the junction. The trail crosses a footbridge over a creek before bending left toward the lake. What will impress you first as you approach Lost Lake is the rich wetland that precedes it, and then, the lily-pads that line its shores. Imagine a flower adapted to live suspended on the surface of the water! A long stem or rootstalk acts like a straw, reaching down into the mud on the bottom of the lake, bringing the large green leaves and showy yellow flowers all the nutrients they need to survive.

This long partially forested valley is just wide enough to contain Lost Lake and the marsh that surrounds it. While many of Yellowstone's features are vast and almost incomprehensible, this is your own personal corner of the universe for the day. Lost Lake is a great place to find yourself, or to lose yourself in the tranquility of the moment.

At the far end of the lake, a small area of burned trees on the distant ridge stands in witness to the day the North Fork fire made a run on the Tower area in 1988. As you can see, the fire barely lapped over the ridge of this secluded valley. Evidence of another powerful force of nature can be seen in the small rockslide at this end of the lake. Water once seeped into the cracks in the cliffs above. As the water froze and expanded, it enlarged these fissures. Fragments of the rock sheared off the mountain and slid down to the ground. This pile of rocks is known in geological terms as a talus slope.

The trail soon leaves the lake and contours around the hillside to the right. The same wetland that makes this small lake so attractive to us, also makes it attractive to moose, who feed on the abundant aquatic plants. As you follow the creek through the narrow ravine beyond Lost Lake, watch closely for these massive creatures, the largest members of the deer family. Give them a wide berth!

Once through the ravine, you'll see the parking area for the petrified tree. The loop trail continues to the right from the end of the parking lot. But by all means, first take a look at the petrified tree. Another large tree once stood next to this one. It was carried away piece by piece by visitors as souvenirs, hence the need for the fence in 1907 to protect the remaining tree. This is a petrified coastal redwood tree. It was buried by mud flows during volcanic eruptions around 50 million years ago. Once the tree was buried, the air spaces within it were plugged by the silica in the water from the volcanic ash. In this way, the tree turned to stone. Yellowstone has the finest petrified forest in the world. If you'd like to see some of these intriguing trees in a more natural setting, hike the trail to the petrified trees, which is described in Chapter 9.

Climbing out of the parking area, you emerge on a sagebrush plateau. As you cross this expanse, you'll be afforded excellent views down the valley to the glaciated peaks of the Absaroka and Beartooth mountains to the east and northeast. Further evidence of the most recent ice age is the large boulders strewn around you. A glacier plucked these rocks from the Beartooth Plateau and carried them along before depositing them here about 13,000 years ago.

On this plateau, a few standing burned trees suggest that flames once swept across this area. If not for these telltale signs, however, you might never know that a cataclysmic fire raged across this landscape in 1988. After fire, grasslands recover quickly in a profusion of wildflowers. Farther down the trail on the left, a dense growth of young lodgepole pines has sprouted up since the fires. Some of their cones are serotinous, which means they need the intense heat of fire to open and release their seeds.

The trail winds in and out of the forest on its way off the plateau, offering good views of the Tower area, below and beyond. Make some noise here, as black bears frequent this area looking for berries in mid- to late summer. Your final descent takes you through a shady glen before reaching the Tower area. Here, you get more of a behind the scenes view of a Park Service maintenance area than you could ever want. Look for orange trail markers. Cross the creek and follow it up to the cabins at Roosevelt Lodge. Don't get lost on the Lost Lake Loop!

I gave heed to the confiding stream, mingled freely with the flowers and light, and shared in the confidence of their exceeding peace.

—Naturalist John Muir, 1874

7

Slough Creek

Get a taste for the old west as you walk an historic wagon road, still in use, to one of the most scenic and beloved spots in all of Yellowstone. Amid Douglas-fir and aspen, glacial boulders, and mountain scenery, this trail follows the meandering waters of Slough Creek through the broad and gentle, flower-laden "First Meadow." *See Plate 7.*

Level of difficulty: Moderate

Distance: 4 miles round trip (6.4 km)

Elevation change: A gain of 400 feet in 1 mile

Duration: 2 - 3 hours

Best time of year: Late May through September. This hike is especially beautiful in fall when the aspen leaves are changing color.

Trailhead: This hike begins from the trailhead near Slough Creek Campground. Drive 6.1 miles (9.8 km) east of Tower Junction and turn left on the entrance road to the campground. Proceed 1.9 miles (3 km) on this gravel road until you reach the trailhead on your right about 0.5 mile (0.8 km) before the campground.

Hiking directions: This trail follows an old road, gradually climbing 400 feet in about a mile. In another mile, the trail reaches Slough Creek and the "First Meadow." Return to the trailhead by the same route.

Special attention: Bears have been known to frequent this area in spring. Be alert and make noise if at any time you can't see in all directions. Also, Slough Creek is a working wagon road, the only means of supplying the remote and historic Silver Tip Ranch north of the park boundary. You may encounter horse parties or horse-drawn wagons along the route. If so, please step off the trail to allow them to safely pass. Enjoy this moment of Americana.

Naturalist notes: Since the trail is the old wagon road to Silver Tip Ranch, shortly past the trailhead you'll encounter a barricade preventing vehicles other than

43

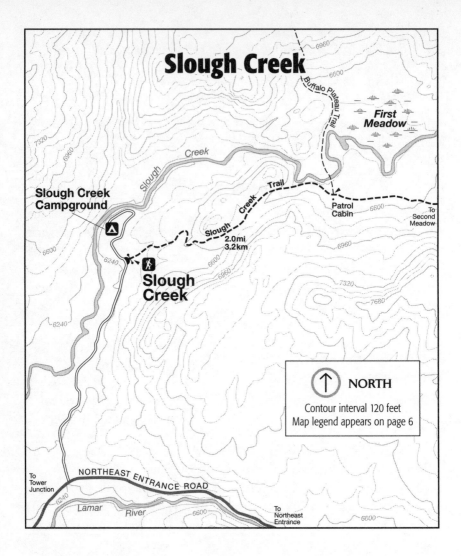

the ranch's from passing through. The trail makes a gradual climb over this wide gravel road through an open forest adorned with wildflowers in mid-summer. Large Douglas-fir trees tower overhead, amid stands of aspen. Some of the wildflowers common along the trail are the wild rose, lupine, sticky and Richardson geranium, and a number of sunflower-like yellow composites, namely the balsamroot, yellow salsify, and the one-flower helianthella.

Scattered on both sides of the trail are some impressively large granite boulders that seem a bit out of place. Imagine these massive rocks riding the wave of the last ice age. Carried by glaciers from faraway places, they were dropped here as the ice melted and began to recede. Much of this granite around you is very old, dating back some 2.7 billion years to the Precambrian Era, when the earth was formed. These ancient rocks from the basement of geologic time are reminders of the powerful forces of nature constantly at work. They also hint at the large glacial valley that awaits you ahead.

Notice that where many of these glacial erratics are strewn, Douglas-fir trees grow. These "nurse rocks" offer enough shade and gather enough moisture at their bases to support a tree in a place that otherwise might be too dry. In the mini-environment they create, new life is born.

Farther along, the trail has a nice open feel, varying between grasslands, Douglas-fir stands, and aspen groves. Aspen trees are a real pleasure. Not common on many of the hiking trails in the park, here they accompany you all the way to Slough Creek and beyond. All of the trees in a stand share the same root system, thus they are clones of one plant. This is perhaps best illustrated during the fall when aspen blanket the Rockies in radiant yellow. As fall approaches, a group of trees will all change color at the same time, while nearby unrelated aspen have yet to turn.

Stand beneath a grove of mature aspen and listen. The gentlest of breezes will cause their leaves to tremble, creating a music of their own, hence the name, quaking aspen. You may notice that this normally white barked tree often has gnarled blackened bark at its base. This is the browse line. Aspen are a popular food with wildlife, particularly elk, who graze on the supple young aspen. If a young plant can get beyond the reach of an inquiring elk, it will grow into a tree. The story of this struggle is recorded in the scarred bark at its base.

After about a mile, the trail levels off. Soon, on your right, you'll pass a narrow wetland. These lush marshy areas with aquatic plants provide excellent habitat for moose.

Looming ahead above the trees, your first glimpse of mountain scenery comes with the ragged outline of 10,691-foot Cutoff Mountain. Before long, the trail begins a gentle descent through the trees, before arriving at a big oxbow bend of Slough Creek. Here is revealed a broad grassy glacial valley through which Slough Creek lazily meanders. Some might call this Shangri La—an imaginary, remote paradise on earth. If this isn't it, it's close, particularly if you're an angler!

Many have called lower Slough Creek "the finest natural cutthroat trout stream in America, if not the world." Its waters drain to the Lamar River, which then flows on to the Yellowstone. The cutthroat have found their way to this spot and so have the fly fishers. You'll see anglers scattered along the banks and in the waters of the creek, trying to land these notoriously hard-to-catch cutthroat. The regulations here are strictly catch and release. Don't worry about being crowded, there's plenty of room for all in this large valley.

Numerous paths lead you down to the water's edge to explore the creek firsthand. In 1874, naturalist John Muir noted the comforting effects of water when he wrote:

I gave heed to the confiding stream, mingled freely with the flowers and light, and shared in the confidence of their exceeding peace.

If you spend some time along this tranquil creek, you may experience this too.

Shortly, you'll reach the 2-mile mark where the Buffalo Plateau Trail (Buffalo Fork) heads to the left, crossing the creek. Just ahead, tucked near the trees to your right, is the Slough Creek backcountry patrol cabin maintained by the National Park Service. Continuing on the main trail, the wagon road climbs a little above the creek through a stand of trees, before emerging at the expansive "First Meadow" of Slough Creek. In spring and fall, elk can often be found in this valley, and in summer moose may ply the waters around the creek.

From here, the wagon road veers away from the creek, continuing on to the Silver Tip Ranch. If you wish to go farther, consider hiking another 1.5 miles, climbing 200 feet over a small knoll, to the creek's "Second Meadow." However near or far you choose to explore, return to the trailhead by the same route.

Before heading back to the trailhead, consider a short side trip. In just a few hundred yards, you'll experience a completely different mood of Slough Creek. From the big oxbow you encountered when you first arrived at the creek, follow the fisherman's trail along the bank, heading downstream away from the meadow. Be careful here, as this is not a maintained trail. It can get a little rough as it winds through and over some large rocks. In a short distance, you'll see a Slough Creek reborn. Where once a meandering body of water flowed, it now crashes through a small narrow canyon, tumbling over large granite boulders strewn in its path. The scene is so different and so surprising that serendipity seems to fill the air. Hopefully, you will also be revitalized on your sojourn to Slough Creek. Return to the trailhead by the same route.

Hubbel went ahead; for a hunt, and upon his return was asked what kind of stream the next creek was. "It's a hell roarer," was his reply, and Hell Roaring is its name to this day.

—Explorer E.S. Topping, 1888

8

Hellroaring Creek

Here's a hike that features a bit of "high" adventure, crossing a suspension bridge over a deep gorge of the Yellowstone River. Then, make your way through an enchanting Douglas-fir forest and big rolling sagebrush country to the banks of Hellroaring Creek. *See Plate 8.*

Level of difficulty: Moderate

Distance: 4 miles round trip (6.4 km)

Elevation change: A loss of 600 feet in 1 mile and subsequent climb up

Duration: 2 - 3 hours

Best time of year: Mid-May through June and September through October (or during the cooler morning and evening hours of summer). This hike is an especially good choice in spring when the higher elevations in the park are still snow-covered.

Trailhead: This hike begins at the parking area for the Hellroaring Trailhead on the north side of the road, just past Floating Island Lake, 3.8 miles (6 km) west of Tower Junction on the Mammoth-Tower Road.

Hiking directions: From the parking area, the trail drops 600 feet in 1 mile passing the Garnet Hill Trail junction, on its way to the suspension bridge over the Yellowstone River. Crossing the bridge, the trail travels another mile, passing the Buffalo Plateau Trail junction, before arriving at Hellroaring Creek. To return, retrace your route across the suspension bridge back to the trailhead.

Naturalist notes: The trail leaves the parking area in an open stand of Douglas-fir trees with sagebrush and a variety of wildflowers in season. In 1988, fire swept through here, burning much of the forest and leaving only a few charred snags still standing. One benefit of fire is that, by removing the forest cover, the views are often vastly improved. This is the case here.

Below, you can see the trail winding down this ridge in search of its first destination, the Yellowstone River. Beyond the river, a grand panorama reveals layer after layer of forest and sagebrush country. Rising to the northeast is the

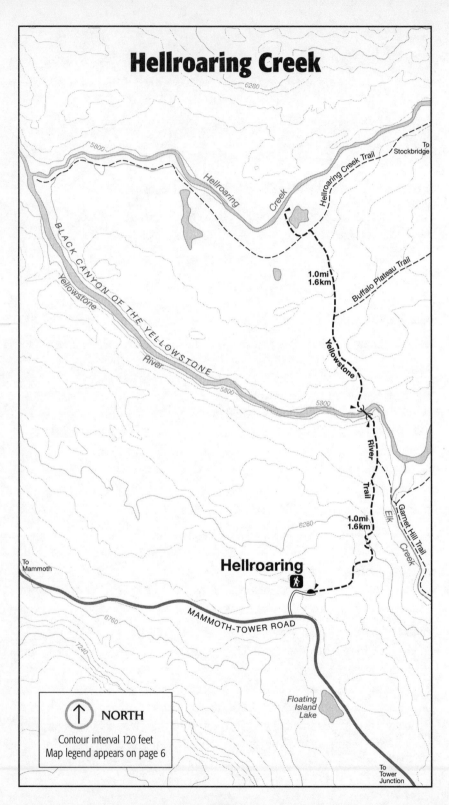

Hellroaring Creek

6280

5800

Hellroaring   *Creek*

Hellroaring Creek Trail

To
Stockbridge

BLACK CANYON OF THE YELLOWSTONE

Yellowstone

**1.0mi
1.6km**

Buffalo Plateau Trail

Yellowstone

River

5800

5800

River

Trail

**1.0mi
1.6km**

Elk

Garnet Hill Trail

Creek

6280

Hellroaring

To
Mammoth

MAMMOTH-TOWER ROAD

6760

7040

*Floating
Island
Lake*

⬆ **NORTH**

Contour interval 120 feet
Map legend appears on page 6

To
Tower
Junction

Buffalo Plateau. To the northwest is a most prominent and unusual peak, Hellroaring Mountain. Looming beyond the creek that shares its name is this rocky cone-shaped mountain with few trees. Hellroaring Mountain is a rarity in Yellowstone. It's one of few mountains in the park made of granite, an anomaly in this otherwise mostly volcanic landscape. Hellroaring is the park's largest granite outcropping, which exposes some of the oldest rock on earth, dating back 2.7 billion years.

More common in Yellowstone is rhyolite, which formed as lava flows covered the area in several massive volcanic eruptions. Rhyolite and granite are chemically equivalent with high concentrations of quartz and feldspar. They differ, however, in how and where they are formed. Rhyolite is created from lava or ash erupting from a volcano that then cools rapidly at the surface. In contrast, granite is an intrusive igneous rock. It forms deep within the earth as molten magma cools very slowly to form the coarse-grained crystals that distinguish this rock. Granite can be brought to the surface during periods of uplift and mountain building such as occurred in the Rockies over the last several million years. This results in mountain chains of rugged grandeur like the Grand Tetons to the south or the Beartooth Plateau, northeast of the park. Yellowstone's history of volcanism has left little room here for granite. Through each successive volcanic period, this ancient rock has been buried deeper beneath layers of lava flows and volcanic debris. That Hellroaring Mountain has survived all this volcanic upheaval to stand here as it does today, gives it its own special charm. Closer views of this timeless mountain of granite await as you near Hellroaring Creek.

From the top of the ridge, the trail begins to wind down through a burned Douglas-fir forest, switchbacking on its 600-foot descent in one mile to the Yellowstone River. On the way down, enjoy the lush growth of grasses and wildflowers. Often blooming here is the showy yellow balsamroot, which prefers open sunny sites. Spring and early summer are the best times to see flowers along the trail. Later in the season, conditions become too dry.

Leveling off, the trail winds through an open forest of unburned Douglas-fir. Continue straight, past the junction with the Garnet Hill Trail on your right. Ahead, the sound of the Yellowstone River grows increasingly louder as you approach the suspension bridge spanning a narrow gorge through which the river flows. This is the beginning of the Black Canyon of the Yellowstone. To fully appreciate the power of the river, cross the suspension bridge and look down on it from above. Don't worry, the bridge is made of steel and is quite sturdy. It's hard to say, though, what's more thrilling—the river below you or the opportunity to walk on this long narrow suspension bridge stretching across the canyon. From this ideal vantage point, the roar of the water is deafening as the mighty Yellowstone thunders through the narrow confines of these rock walls. While exploring the lower stretches of the Black Canyon in 1870, Lt. Gustavus Doane recorded his own impressions of the river's response to its plight: *Standing on the brink of the chasm, the heavy roaring of the imprisoned river comes to the ear only in a sort of hollow hungry growl.* Indeed, it does seem as though this great river has been forced into a space too small to contain it. The result, however, is most impressive.

Across the bridge, the trail winds through a few trees and into an area of open sagebrush. Beyond, there's a short gentle climb between two wooded hills as you enter a cool dark forest of large Douglas-firs. Giant boulders are scattered everywhere, with grasses and wildflowers growing in the dappled light of the trees. On a warm day, the shade of this forest is quite inviting, beckoning you to linger awhile. Through the years, the children who attend the park's residential environmental education program, Expedition: Yellowstone!, have come to affectionately refer to this spot as "the Enchanted Forest." Sitting on the large rocks in the shade of these big trees, they're often asked to record their impressions. Charly Sue Cook, a fifth grader from Tetonia Elementary School in Idaho, wrote of this place: *The Enchanted Forest is quiet and peaceful. The forest is so quiet that you can hear your heart beat…I love this forest because it is beautiful. I just hope it lasts forever.*

Before you continue, take some time in the cool shade amid the rock and wood. After a brief respite, leave the shelter of this dark forest. The trail emerges from the woods onto a wholly different landscape—a broad, rolling terrain of sage-covered hills. Just ahead on the right, the trail meets the junction with the Buffalo Plateau Trail. Stay left and head across this open country filled with large sagebrush and strewn with more boulders. You may have noticed some of these large rocks at the suspension bridge and in the enchanted forest. They are wonderful examples of the power of ice to move rock. Called "glacial erratics," they were deposited when glaciers from the last ice age began to melt and retreat, littering the land with the rock they'd been carrying from distant places. Like Hellroaring Mountain looming ahead to the north, they are also composed of granite, but they began their journey in the faraway Beartooth Plateau northeast of the park.

In about 0.5 mile, the trail descends gently to a junction. At this intersection, turn left (toward campsites 2H2+2H4). In several hundred yards, the trail to Hellroaring Creek veers right and skirts around a small intermittent pond or glacial "kettle." In this spot, a large block of retreating ice was buried beneath glacial soils. As the ice melted, the earth collapsed, producing a shallow depression that today holds water until fall. Surrounded by the dry, sagebrush-covered terrain is this "glacial oasis"—a pond filled with a host of water-loving plants and bird life.

Beyond this little pond lie the waters of Hellroaring Creek. This lovely tree-lined stream is home to the native cutthroat trout and a popular destination for anglers. Find a comfortable rock to enjoy the serenity that's found only in flowing water. If it's a warm day, here's a good spot to shed your boots and cool your feet in these refreshing waters. Though it may be tempting to ford the creek here, don't try it. The current can be quite swift.

Once you've explored the creek and its surroundings, retrace your route back across the suspension bridge to the trailhead. Pace yourself for the 600-foot climb you must make in the final mile.

If you wish to hike farther, you can follow the trails that parallel the creek. Just before you arrive at the creek, you'll see two trails, one heading left and the other, right. To the left, you follow Hellroaring Creek downstream for about a mile to where it joins the Yellowstone River. At this confluence, the trail ends in a beautiful sandy beach. If you choose to head in the other direction, turn right and hike upstream for a couple of miles to where you cross the creek on a stock bridge. Either way, return to the trailhead by the same route.

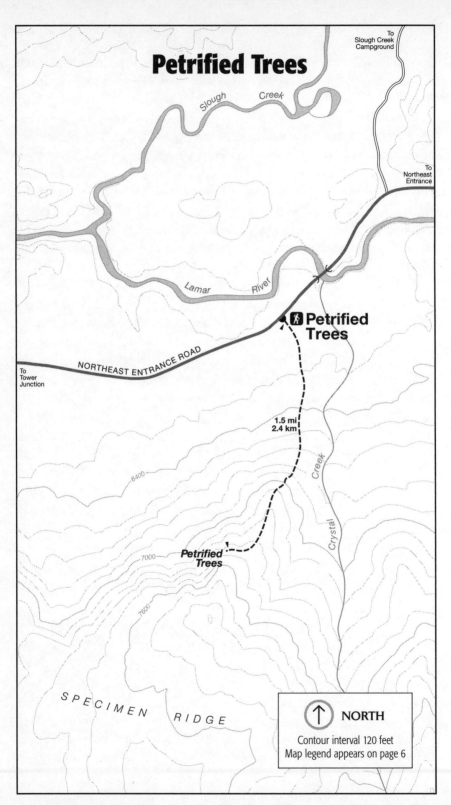

Petrified Trees

To
Slough Creek
Campground

To
Northeast
Entrance

Slough *Creek*

Lamar *River*

🚶 **Petrified Trees**

NORTHEAST ENTRANCE ROAD

To
Tower
Junction

**1.5 mi
2.4 km**

Crystal *Creek*

6400

Petrified Trees

7000

7600

S P E C I M E N   R I D G E

⬆ **NORTH**

Contour interval 120 feet
Map legend appears on page 6

I'll show you peetrified trees a-growing,
with peetrified birds on 'em a-singing peetrified songs.
—Mountain man Jim Bridger, 1897

Petrified Trees

Yellowstone contains so many wonders, the fact that it has the largest petrified forest in the world goes almost unnoticed! Although it's possible to drive to a petrified tree in the park, it's much more interesting to encounter them on the path less taken. This short, but very steep, trail takes you to a few of the most impressive of the petrified trees, with commanding views of the Lamar River, Slough Creek, and the surrounding mountain ranges. Enjoy these fascinating trees, immortalized in myth and stone. *See Plate 9.*

Level of difficulty: Strenuous

Distance: 3 miles round trip (4.8 km)

Elevation change: A gain of 1,200 feet in 1.5 miles

Duration: 2 - 3 hours

Best time of year: Late May through June and September through October (or during the cooler morning and evening hours of summer).

Trailhead: This hike begins at the pullout on the south side of the road 5.3 miles (8.5 km) east of Tower Junction and 0.2 miles (0.3 km) west of the Lamar River bridge on the Northeast Entrance Road. Do not confuse this with the Specimen Ridge Trailhead.

Hiking directions: There are a number of fossil forests in Yellowstone and a number of trails that will take you to them. This is one of the shortest, most direct routes. The trail starts on the faint remnant of an old service road, now barely visible. After about 100 yards, it veers off the road to the right on a trail through a sagebrush flat. The trail climbs gradually to a small group of trees. From here, the trail begins to steepen. Farther up the hillside, you reach a larger forest. Here, the trail forks. Continue to the right, up the northern ridge of the hillside. At this point, the trail gets strikingly steep. After making the climb, the trail emerges on a plateau near a large petrified tree lying on its side. Continue along the ridge line, gradually climbing several grassy benches. Along the way, several unofficial or "social" trails lead to various specimens. Stay on the lower trail, which leads toward a dense forest on the north slope. This forest is to the right of the large rock outcropping and the burned trees higher up the mountain. Follow the trail through the forest until it suddenly opens up at the petrified trees. Return to the trailhead via the same route.

Special attention: This trail is extremely steep in sections. Wear good hiking boots for traction and watch your footing on loose rocks. Remember, collecting petrified wood is prohibited by law in national parks. Please leave these most unusual specimens in place for others to enjoy.

Naturalist notes: Once off the service road, you'll see the trail winding up the hillside in front of you toward your destination. In spring and early summer, it passes through a small boggy wetland. A short detour may be required around the marsh to keep your boots dry. Soon, you begin to climb gradually up a series of grassy hills or benches toward the crest of the ridge.

Before long, you'll reach several Douglas-fir trees. Here, the trail steepens, continuing uphill into a larger stand of Douglas-fir. In this forest, there could be a point of some confusion. For reasons that you'll soon clearly understand, people have made a social trail off to the left in an attempt to find a less arduous ascent to the top. Resist the temptation to follow it. It won't take you where you want to go, and you may never find the famous trees. Instead, continue to the right up the steeper route.

From here, the trail becomes inhumanly steep, for a mercifully short distance. There will be several occasions to pause and catch your breath. Enjoy the fine views of the mountains behind you and the many wildflowers along the way. Ponder the legends of the fossil forests.

The mountain men, trapping beaver in this region in the early 1800s, told of a great medicine man of the Crow Nation who once invoked a curse on this mountain. As the story goes, from that moment on, everything was petrified in place. The animals were halted in their tracks and turned to stone. Fur-trapper and famous teller of tall tales, Jim Bridger, told General Nelson A. Miles: *Come with me to the Yellowstone...and I'll show you peetrified trees a-growing, with peetrified birds on 'em a-singing peetrified songs.*

Army Engineer, Captain Hiram Chittenden, recalled hearing of this dubious phenomenon, ...*flowers are blooming in colors of crystal and birds soar with wings spread in motionless flight...while the sun and the moon shine with petrified light!*

Fortunately, the trail soon flattens out, bringing you back to your senses. You may have seen several small petrified logs and stumps as you climbed through this last whimsical discourse, but by now you should see a large petrified tree, lying on its side, perhaps 4-5 feet in diameter. If this is the only petrified tree you find, it will have been worth the effort. Feel free to examine it more closely, but watch your footing on the loose rocks around it.

There are a few more grassy hills to climb before you reach your destination. Here again, people have made trails to many of the different specimens. Look for the Douglas-fir forest to the right of the large rock outcropping and the burned trees near the top of the mountain.

This part of the trail has somewhat of a fairy tale feel, following along a densely wooded, precipitous hillside toward the proverbial light at the end of the tunnel. Immediately upon emerging from the forest, you see the great trees. Not only are the trees an incredible sight to behold, so are the views of the valley and the mountains beyond. Keep your eyes on the ground, however, if you wish to observe the trees more closely. The incline is steep and the rocks are shaky.

The massive stump before you is a redwood tree, about 26 feet in circumference, which towered several hundred feet tall when it was alive. Two smaller petrified trees stand below it. Taking a cautious walk below the trees, you'll see that their root systems and tree rings remain remarkably intact.

Yellowstone's fossil forest is world renowned, in part, because many of the trees are still standing, having been engulfed and entombed by mud flows after volcanic eruptions 50 million years ago. Once the trees were buried, the air spaces within them were plugged by the silica in the water from the volcanic ash; hence, the trees turned to stone. Since individual cells are preserved, scientists can tell what kind of forests once grew here. Most of the trees in the 40-square-mile fossil forest are redwoods. Others, however, are even more surprising. Imagine a Yellowstone with magnolia, avocado, and dogwood trees! The lessons locked in stone here reveal an ancient climate much warmer than today's.

After your trip back in geological time, retrace your steps down to the valley floor, enjoying the excellent views of the rugged peaks to the northeast.

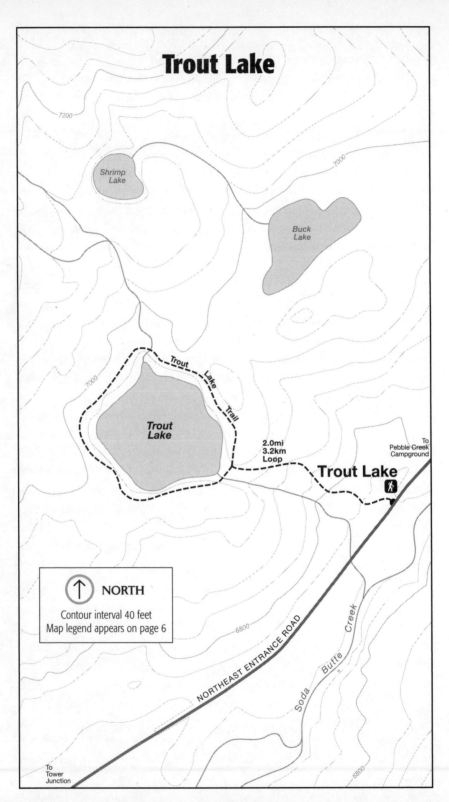

Trout Lake

Shrimp Lake

Buck Lake

Trout Lake Trail

Trout Lake

2.0mi
3.2km
Loop

Trout Lake

To
Pebble Creek
Campground

↑ NORTH

Contour interval 40 feet
Map legend appears on page 6

NORTHEAST ENTRANCE ROAD

Soda Butte Creek

7200

7000

7000

6800

6800

To
Tower
Junction

The joys of mountain trouting are largely owing to the surroundings.
Writer George Shields, 1892

10

Trout Lake

Though long known to anglers, this remarkable short hike still remains a well kept secret to many in Yellowstone. Those who make the effort to hike this trail will be greatly rewarded. Not only is the scenery extraordinary, but this small lake has an important story to tell. If you'd like to get a closeup view of cutthroat trout, this is one of the best places in the park to do so. *See Plate 10.*

Level of difficulty: Easy

Distance: 2 miles round trip (3.2 km)

Elevation change: A gain of 120 feet in 0.6 miles

Duration: 1 - 2 hours

Best time of year: Mid-May through late June is the best time to observe the trout spawn, but this is a pleasant hike any time from spring through fall.

Trailhead: This hike begins at the pullout on the north side of the road, 1.8 miles (2.9 km) west of Pebble Creek Campground and 18.5 miles (29.6 km) east of Tower Junction on the Northeast Entrance Road.

Hiking directions: The trail climbs for a short distance as it winds up a steep slope through a forest before reaching Trout Lake. The trail continues around this small lake, returning to the trailhead by the same route.

Naturalist notes: While catching your breath on this short but steep hike, you'll notice that you're in an open forest of spruce and fir. Since 80 percent of the trees in Yellowstone are lodgepole pines, this is somewhat of a rare treat. The Douglas-fir and Engelmann spruce are among the most graceful of the evergreens. The lush understory, full of a wide array of wildflowers in spring, draws you up the hill hardly noticing the elevation gain. The sound of the creek rushing beside you is fitting music for this colorful scene. The stream is only occasionally in view, but its bright tones lure you farther up the path.

The trail winds up the mountainside, twisting and turning, until soon, it takes a sharp right turn over a small rise. Trout Lake appears suddenly and steeply below you. Your first view of the lake is of the clear green waters that rest calmly behind a small dam under a rustic footbridge before they cascade down the mountain. A few steps farther down the hill, the whole scene unfolds before you.

When George Shields reported in the magazine, *American Game Fishes,* in 1892 that *the joys of mountain trouting are largely owing to the surroundings,* he must have been referring to a place like this. This small lake is nestled in some of the most striking mountain scenery Yellowstone has to offer. The rocky cliffs of Mount Hornaday rise impressively above. If you're hiking this trail in spring, you may see the long waterfall that drops down the face of this rugged peak in the distance, but this ephemeral cascade disappears later in the summer.

Take the short walk around the lake. Almost halfway around, you cross a small log bridge over the creek that is the inlet to the lake. If you hadn't already known of it, you'll be surprised by the stunning spectacle of the spawning trout. Between mid-May and mid-June, depending on the year, hundreds of trout crowd this shallow stream to lay their eggs. Twisting and slapping their tails, the females dig small holes, called redds, in which they deposit their eggs. Swimming beside the females, the males then fertilize the eggs. In addition to the red, gash-like stripe on the throat that gives these fish their name, the cutthroat trout also display a bright red patch behind their gills during the mating season. While observing these brilliantly colored fish, it's almost impossible to imagine the many obstacles they've had to overcome in their turbulent past.

This lovely little lake was originally known as Fish Lake. Appropriately named, it represents the many changes that have occurred over the years in how fish are perceived and managed in Yellowstone. When the park was established in 1872, it was the first national park in the world. The idea of preserving fish and wildlife was relatively new and was not readily accepted by all. The miners in nearby Cooke City, Montana, used this lake as their personal source for trout. The native cutthroat were taken by any and all means possible. They were netted, they were speared, they were even blasted out with gunpowder. The first park superintendents had neither the power nor the authority to stop these horrific practices.

When the National Park Service was created in 1916, another chapter in the history of Trout Lake and of fisheries management was written. In a park established "for the benefit and enjoyment of the people," early park managers sought not necessarily to preserve native species, but rather to provide fish, fish, and more fish for people to catch. A hatchery was built at Trout Lake to transplant eggs from these fish to other park waters. In 1934, a non-native fish, the rainbow trout, was introduced here for the same purpose. While no genetic studies have been done on these fish, it's widely believed that the two fish interbred, creating the hybrid "cutbow."

In the following decades, attitudes toward nature began to change across the country and in the national parks. The emphasis shifted from merely providing recreational experiences for visitors to preserving native species for their own sake, regardless of their usefulness to people.

The mission of the National Park Service is to "conserve the wildlife" and "to provide for the enjoyment of the same, in such manner and by such means as will leave them unimpaired for the enjoyment of future generations." Today, Trout Lake represents this balance between human use and wildlife preservation. You may fish in the lake, though it's catch and release, with no fishing at the inlet until July 15. Now, with sound fisheries management policies in place, we can hope that this amazing springtime ritual will be here for future generations to enjoy. According to local legend, these huge fish are known to be wary and hard to catch. Perhaps they have a long memory of the past.

Whether you fish or not, take time to relax along the shore and enjoy the dramatic views of this small lake with the sheer mountains behind it. Bring a book or take a nap. Consider the significance of a nation's commitment to valuing wildlife and wildlands.

Now that you've learned this well kept secret, you're likely to return. The short hike back down to the road provides even more incredible views of the Absaroka Mountains.

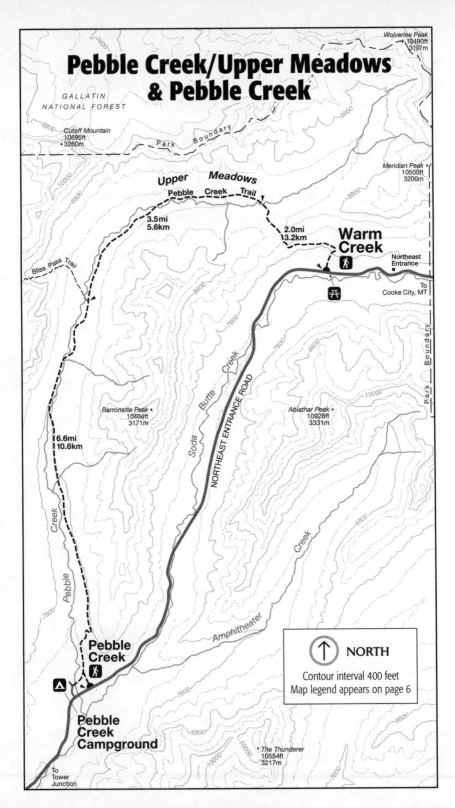

Pebble Creek/Upper Meadows & Pebble Creek

GALLATIN
NATIONAL FOREST

Wolverine Peak •
10490ft
3197m

Cutoff Mountain
10695ft
• 3260m

Park   Boundary

Meridian Peak •
10500ft
3200m

Upper   Meadows
Pebble   Creek   Trail

3.5mi
5.6km

2.0mi
13.2km

**Warm
Creek**

Northeast
Entrance

Bliss Pass Trail

To
Cooke City, MT

Barronette Peak •
10404ft
3171m

Soda   Butte   Creek

NORTHEAST ENTRANCE ROAD

Abiathar Peak •
10928ft
3331m

Park   Boundary

6.6mi
10.6km

Pebble   Creek

Creek

**Pebble
Creek**

Amphitheater

	NORTH
Contour interval 400 feet	
Map legend appears on page 6	

**Pebble
Creek
Campground**

• The Thunderer
10554ft
3217m

To
Tower
Junction

...Nature's sources never fail. Like a generous host, she offers here brimming cups in endless variety, served in a grand hall, the sky its ceiling, the mountains its walls, decorated with glorious paintings and enlivened with bands of music ever playing. —Naturalist John Muir, 1885

11

Pebble Creek/Upper Meadows & Pebble Creek

Far off the beaten path, this hike reveals some of the most captivating Rocky Mountain scenery in the park. As you ascend to a secluded glacial valley to explore the wildflower-laden Upper Meadows of Pebble Creek, the wilderness world of Yellowstone unfolds amid the rugged grandeur of some of the park's tallest peaks. *See Plate 11.*

Pebble Creek/Upper Meadows

Level of difficulty: Strenuous

Distance: 4 miles round trip (6.4 km)

Elevation change: A gain of 1,000 feet in 1.5 miles

Duration: 3 - 4 hours

Pebble Creek

Level of difficulty: Strenuous

Distance: 12.1 miles (19.4 km) one way. *This hike requires a shuttle back to the trailhead.*

Elevation change: A gain of 1,000 feet in 1.5 miles

Duration: 6 - 8 hours

Best time of year: Mid-July through September. Depending how far you choose to go, this hike could require 1 to 4 fords of Pebble Creek. Since high water can persist on Pebble Creek through early July, consider hiking this trail later in the summer and fall, when the water level has dropped, making the crossings easier.

Trailhead: This hike begins at the Warm Creek Trailhead, 1.2 miles (1.9 km) west of the Northeast Entrance and 28.2 (45.5 km) miles east of Tower Junction on the north side of the road. Do not confuse this with the Pebble Creek

Trailhead located near the entrance to Pebble Creek Campground, which is the end of this 12-mile shuttle hike.

Hiking directions: Two hiking options begin from this trailhead: hiking into the Upper Meadows and back or continuing all the way down Pebble Creek. For both, the trail begins by climbing steeply up 1,000 feet in 1.5 miles before descending 200 feet to the Upper Meadows and the banks of Pebble Creek. Ford the creek and explore as much of this scenic valley as you wish. Return to the trailhead by the same route.

For those continuing on, hike the length of the meadow to a second crossing of Pebble Creek. After making the ford, follow the trail as it parallels the creek through a spruce and fir forest. At the 5.5-mile marker, the trail intersects the Bliss Pass Trail on the right. Continue straight for an additional 6.6 miles to the where the trail ends at Pebble Creek Campground. Along the way, two more fords of Pebble Creek are required before the trail begins to switchback down to the campground. Near the campground, the trail splits. The right fork leads to the campground and the left fork takes you to the Pebble Creek Trailhead on the Northeast Entrance Road.

Special attention: Bears have been known to frequent this area in spring. Be alert and make noise if at anytime you can't see clearly in all directions. Use extreme caution when fording the creek.

Naturalist notes: This trail begins in the lovely setting of a spruce and fir forest not far from the banks of Soda Butte Creek. The first part of the hike is very steep, climbing a literally breathtaking 1,000 feet in 1.5 miles. Fortunately, the incredible scenery along the way gives you the perfect excuse to stop and rest often, allowing you take in these extraordinary views between breaths.

Initially, the trail climbs through a stately forest of Engelmann spruce, Douglas-fir, and subalpine fir, with a lush understory of grasses and flowers. At times, the trail levels off awhile and then continues climbing. Eventually, you'll emerge from the forest to cross a very sheer talus slope of loose rock. From this vantage point you'll obtain great views of the mountain range in which you are hiking—the rugged, 50 million year old Absaroka Range. Barronette Peak lies ahead, and towering Abiathar Peak stands to your left. Tucked between the two, stretches the forested valley of Soda Butte Creek. Imagine massive ice sheets filling the space between the mountains, scouring and carving the U-shaped valley you see below.

These mountain views accompany you back into the forest for the final steep ascent, with the aid of a few short switchbacks. When you arrive at the pass in the mountains, you'll find that the hard work has been done. The trail begins a somewhat steep descent of about 200 feet to the meadows below. You'll soon be richly rewarded for your efforts when you emerge from the open stands of spruce and fir to the banks of Pebble Creek. With all the rounded river rocks in the stream bed, it's easy to see how it got its name. Carefully, find a safe place to ford the creek.

Safely across, watch your whole world change as the scene opens up into the long expansive Upper Meadows through which Pebble Creek flows. The trail follows the creek downstream, running the length of these meadows for the next couple of miles, offering incredible views of the many mountains bounding this huge glacial valley.

In the 1830s, mountain man Osborne Russell wrote of a similar scene in the describing nearby Lamar Valley. His words could have just as easily applied to the Upper Meadows of Pebble Creek: *There is something in the wild romantic scenery of this valley which I cannot describe; but the impressions made upon my mind…One evening as the sun was gently gliding behind the western mountain and casting its gigantic shadows across the vale were such as time can never efface from my memory…for my own part I almost wished I could spend the remainder of my days in a place like this where happiness and contentment seemed to reign in wild romantic splendor.*

Wild romantic splendor! Russell captured this part of Yellowstone well. The scenery that surrounds you here is simply superb. Ahead to the west, foreboding Cutoff Mountain dominates, while to the left and south, Abiathar Peak continues to stand guard, towering above the neighboring forests. Behind you, marking the park boundary, are Wolverine Peak to the northeast and Sunset and Meridian peaks to the east. These three mountains were not in the park's original 1872 boundary, but were part of a 1929 addition that expanded the park's northeast corner to include Pebble Creek's headwaters. On a map, you'll notice how the park boundary here deviates from the straight political lines drawn historically around the park. This meandering border includes the upper realms of the Pebble Creek watershed, defining the park boundary in a more ecologically appropriate way.

Beneath these giant volcanic peaks are the Upper Meadows. Gentle and serene, they lie in great contrast to the sheer mountain walls around them. Throughout July and early August, wildflowers grace the valley floor, blooming profusely in an assortment of shapes and colors. Small streams trickle out of the mountains, flowing across the meadows on their way to the larger Pebble Creek. In the morning and evening hours of summertime, moose have been known to graze on grasses and willows at the water's edge. Herds of elk congregate here in autumn. Take time to enjoy the many wonders of these Upper

Meadows, before venturing back down to civilization.

If you wish to make this a longer hike of 12 miles, you can walk the length of Pebble Creek back to the campground. Once past the Upper Meadows, the trail is not quite so open as it descends along the creek through a mostly forested valley. Though you lose the grand views, it still makes for a delightful long day hike.

To continue, hike to the western end of the Upper Meadows. Ford the creek for a second time and follow the trail through a forested area to the junction with the Bliss Pass Trail on the right at the 5.5-mile mark. Continue straight as the trail travels an additional 6.6 miles back to the campground. As you hike through a forest of lodgepole pine, spruce, and fir, Pebble Creek comes in and out of view. Two more fords of the creek are required, occurring within a mile of each other. Beyond the last ford, the trail travels through more forest before opening into a small meadow, revealing more mountain scenery highlighted by a spectacular view of the Thunderer to the southeast.

Beyond the meadow, the trail enters a beautiful open Douglas-fir forest. Here, you'll descend a number of switchbacks as the trail drops 500 feet and turns sharply left, again paralleling the creek below on your right as you arrive near Pebble Creek Campground. Just above the campground the trail forks. To the left, you can hike to the Pebble Creek Trailhead located near the campground entrance on the Northeast Entrance Road, or, just ahead to the right, the trail ends in the campground.

*...Where mist-nourished flowers and carpets of green
Commingling in bowers like Eden are seen.*
—Yellowstone Superintendent Philetus W. Norris, 1883

Cascade Lake &
Cascade Lake/Observation Peak

This trail near Canyon Village will usher you over spring-fed creeks and through expansive meadows to a little lake often frequented by moose. In early summer, wildflowers adorn the meadows. Those heading up to the top of Observation Peak will find few people and great views of Yellowstone from a lofty perch. *See Plate 12.*

Cascade Lake

Level of difficulty: Moderate

Distance: 5 miles round trip (8 km)

Elevation change: Minimal

Duration: 2 - 3 hours

Cascade Lake/Observation Peak

Level of difficulty: Strenuous

Distance: 11 miles round trip (17.6 km)

Elevation change: A gain of 1,400 feet in 3 miles

Duration: 5 - 7 hours

Best time of year: July through September. In spring and early summer, the meadows around Cascade Lake can be very wet and snow may persist on Observation Peak. July is optimal for wildflowers.

Trailhead: This hike begins from the Cascade Lake Picnic Area on the west side of the road, 1.4 miles (2.2 km) north of Canyon Junction. Do not confuse this with the Cascade Creek Trail located 0.5 mile west of Canyon Junction.

Hiking directions: From the trailhead sign on the west side of the picnic area, this hike skirts through forest and meadow before encountering the Cascade Creek Trail on your left. Stay to the right and continue for about a mile to Cascade Lake. A number of paths take you down to explore the lakeshore.

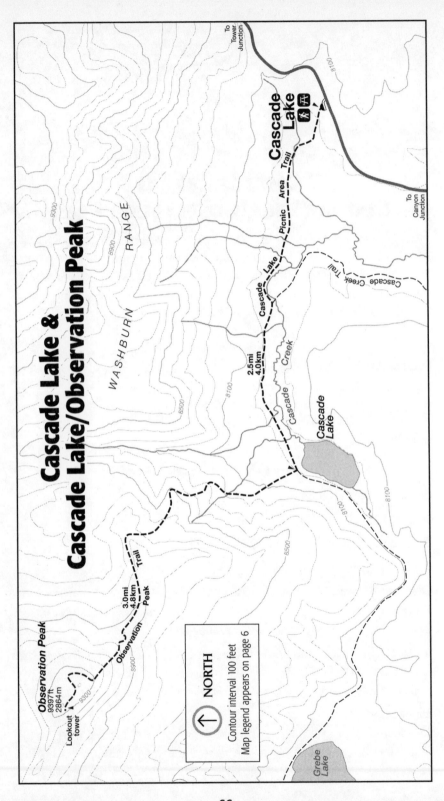

Cascade Lake &
Cascade Lake/Observation Peak

WASHBURN RANGE

Observation Peak
9397ft
2864m

Lookout tower

3.0mi
4.8km

Observation Peak Trail

2.5mi
4.0km

Cascade Creek

Cascade Lake

Cascade Lake Trail

Cascade Creek Trail

Picnic Area Trail

Cascade
Lake

Cascade Lake

Grebe Lake

To Tower Junction

To Canyon Junction

NORTH

Contour interval 100 feet
Map legend appears on page 6

Return to the trailhead by the same route.

For those hiking on to Observation Peak, go to the trail junction that is located on the northwest end of the lake, near where the trail first encounters the lakeshore. Begin the 3-mile 1,400-foot climb to the summit. Return to the trailhead by the same route.

Special attention: It can be cold and windy on Observation Point, even on days when it's warm at lower elevations. Be prepared with warm clothes, and wind- and raingear. Bears have been known to frequent the Cascade Lake Trail in spring and Observation Peak in the fall. Be alert and make noise if at any time you can't see clearly in all directions. The exposed slope up Observation Peak can be very hot and dry. Bring plenty of water.

Naturalist notes: From the picnic area, the trail passes briefly through an old lodgepole pine forest before emerging into a meadow. In the distance, Observation Peak comes into view. This forest was affected by the mosaic burn pattern typical of the fires of 1988. Driven by high winds, the flames seared some trees while blowing past others. For the next mile, you'll pass in and out of these burned areas paralleling the edge of the forest on your right. However, what dominates the landscape and captures the imagination most here are the meadows. The trail crosses four small spring-fed streams that traverse the meadows, some by footbridge, some by log, and others by a good strong leap! Don't worry, they're easy crossings.

In July, you'll witness wonderful displays of wildflowers here. Within the many shades of the green grasses is a sea of evolving colors—silvery blue lupine, the deep purple larkspur, paintbrush in a palette of reds, oranges, and pinks, and the rosy-hued sticky geranium, to name but a few. Look for the delicate low-lying white phlox on the open slopes and the yellow heartleaf arnica in the forest. Scattered across these meadows is a plant standing high above the rest: the tall and stalky showy green gentian. Its leaves sprout up year after year until the conditions are perfect for it to bloom. It blooms only once in a lifetime and then it dies. So, if you see one, it's a special occasion!

The trail bends to the right, leading into a narrow forested area. Soon, to your left, you're joined by Cascade Creek as it winds through the trees amid a lush understory. Yellowstone's second Superintendent, Philetus W. Norris, sought out this place, which he called "the glen of the Cascade," as his personal place of retreat. In 1883, he wrote a tribute to it:

> *Unselfish I've struggled to benefit men,*
> *Regretless I leave them, my refuge the glen,*
> *Where mist-nourished flowers and carpets of green*
> *Commingling in bowers like Eden are seen.*

Perhaps like Norris, you'll find refuge on this path.

On the left, you'll meet the junction with the Cascade Creek Trail. Stay to the right and continue through this forest of lodgepoles mixed with some large spruce and fir. From here, it's a little more than a mile to Cascade Lake. The trail moves away from the edge of the creek, though paralleling it all the way to the lake. In time, the forest gives way to reveal the massive meadow bounding Cascade Lake. In the middle of this broad and long meadow, you'll pass a spur trail heading off to the left, leading to a backcountry campsite.

Ahead, you'll be treated to your first views of the 36-acre Cascade Lake. The fires in 1988 burned through the once dense forest down to the lakeshore. Cascade Creek flows from the north side of the lake to its dramatic destiny. Beyond the meadow, it tumbles 129 feet over the north rim of the Grand Canyon of the Yellowstone as Crystal Falls. You can see this grand performance on the North Rim of the Canyon Trail. Crystal Falls creates an insurmountable obstacle for fish! Both Cascade Creek and Lake were naturally barren of fish. Today, Cascade Lake is home to two of Yellowstone's native fish, the popular cutthroat trout and the rare and beautiful grayling. Stocking efforts, as early as 1889, introduced the cutthroat into the lake. During the 1930-1950s, grayling were added from a hatchery operated on nearby Grebe Lake.

Spend some time exploring this pretty little mountain lake. Enjoy the lily pads floating near the lake's inlet to the south. Moose are sometimes seen grazing on the aquatic plants around the lake. Keep a look out for this charismatic critter. If Cascade Lake is your destination for today, after your explorations, retrace your steps back to the trailhead.

If you're heading to Observation Peak, go to the trail junction at the northwest end of the lake. The trail climbs away from Cascade Lake through some open country, passing a path leading to a backcountry campsite to the right. Continue straight into a large spruce and fir forest. Much of the forest on Observation Peak burned in 1988, creating a profusion of grasses and wildflowers. The trail climbs in and out of burned and unburned spruce forests, crossing a creek on a footbridge, before emerging to a point overlooking Cascade Lake. Climbing a series of switchbacks, the trail gets steeper and rockier, leveling off occasionally before making the final ascent to the top. Along the way, look for a magenta colored Indian paintbrush at your feet and whitebark pine overhead. This high elevation pine tells you you're near your goal.

At 9,397 feet, Observation Peak is part of the Washburn Range, volcanic mountains that erupted 50 million years ago. On this narrow, windswept rocky perch, amid volcanic boulders and a few gnarled trees, sits an old lookout tower, braving the wind and cold. At this elevation, you, too, will be braving the elements since this lookout is currently boarded up and closed to the public. During the first half of the summer, you'll be crossing over remnants of snow from the past winter as you make your way to the top.

Like its more famous neighbor, Mount Washburn, Observation Peak offers many of the same breathtaking views with one notable exception—people. Far less traveled, you'll have the trail mostly to yourself. To the west stands the Gallatin Range and to the north Cook and Folsom peaks of the Washburn Range. The sweeping view south takes in much of Yellowstone. Just below the summit lies Grebe Lake, with Wolf Lake to your right. Beyond are the volcanic Central Plateau, the Red Mountains, and farther still, the Grand Tetons. Closer to the south lie Hayden Valley and the Yellowstone River, which flows from Yellowstone Lake in the far distance.

The Observation Point Trail is one of those hikes that offers great views both coming and going. On your way back down the mountain, you are afforded magnificent views of the Grand Canyon of the Yellowstone and the rugged Absaroka Range that bounds the park's east side. Once back at Cascade Lake, turn left toward the meadows and continue back to the trailhead.

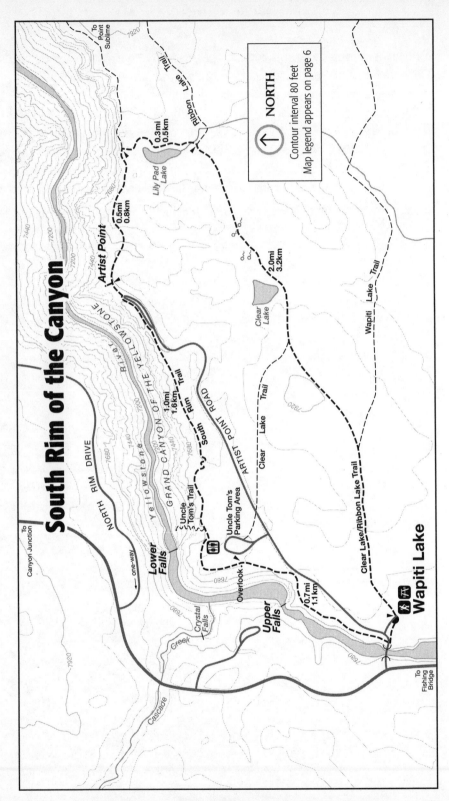

South Rim of the Canyon

NORTH

Contour interval 80 feet
Map legend appears on page 6

To Point Sublime

Ribbon Lake Trail

0.3mi
0.5km

Lily Pad Lake

0.5mi
0.8km

Artist Point

2.0mi
3.2km

Clear Lake

Wapiti Lake Trail

GRAND CANYON OF THE YELLOWSTONE

Yellowstone River

1.0mi
1.6km

South Rim Trail

Clear Lake Trail

ARTIST POINT ROAD

Uncle Tom's Trail

Uncle Tom's Parking Area

Clear Lake/Ribbon Lake Trail

Lower Falls

NORTH RIM DRIVE

Canyon Junction

one-way

Crystal Falls

Overlook

Upper Falls

0.7mi
1.1km

Wapiti Lake

Cascade Creek

To Fishing Bridge

*...language is inadequate to convey a just conception...
of this masterpiece of nature's handiwork.*
—Explorer David Folsom, 1869

13

South Rim of the Canyon

From the South Rim, you experience some of the most extraordinary scenery in the nation, if not the world. The Upper and Lower Falls of the Yellowstone River plunge powerfully into the canyon below. The kaleidoscope of colors on the steep walls of this canyon make it truly "grand." A loop trail brings you back past mysterious mudpots and several small lakes before returning to the trailhead. *See Plate 13.*

Level of difficulty: Moderate

Distance: 4.5-mile loop (7.2 km)

Elevation change: A gain of 120 feet in 0.5 mile

Duration: 2 - 3 hours (add another 45 minutes if taking the side trip down Uncle Tom's Trail)

Best time of year: June through September.

Trailhead: This hike begins at the Wapiti Lake Picnic Area and Trailhead. Drive 2.3 miles south of Canyon Junction and turn left on Artist Point Road. The Wapiti Lake Picnic Area is just across the bridge on the right side of the road. The trail leaves from the picnic area. Do not take the Wapiti Lake or Howard Eaton trail on the far side of the parking area.

Hiking directions: Follow the wide paved path from the picnic area for the short distance to Artist Point Road. Do not go across the bridge. Carefully cross the road and take the trail that starts next to the bridge. The trail parallels the river for 0.7 mile gaining a little elevation before it reaches the overlook of the Upper Falls at Uncle Tom's parking area. From this point, do not take the path to the parking lot to the right, but continue straight along the canyon rim. After a few switchbacks, you'll pass another trail on the right, which also leads back to the parking area. Bear left. Soon you'll arrive at the junction with Uncle Tom's Trail. If you choose to make this side trip, turn left. If not, continue straight for 1 mile to the Artist Point parking area. The trail resumes on the far side of the parking lot. In about 100 yards, you'll reach Artist Point. Beyond Artist Point, the trail leaves from the far end of the lower viewing area and continues along the canyon rim. In 0.5 mile, you'll meet the trail junction for Lily Pad Lake. Turn right here. In 0.3 mile, past Lily Pad Lake, you'll encounter the junction with the Ribbon Lake Trail. Turn right and proceed 0.5 mile to Clear Lake. Just beyond Clear Lake, you come to a "Y" junction. Continue straight for 1.3 miles, back to the Wapiti Trailhead.

Special attention: The canyon walls are steep and unforgiving. Keep a safe distance from the rims.

Naturalist notes: You can drive to a number of prominent overlooks of the canyon and falls, but why not follow the Yellowstone River on its incredible journey? From the Chittenden Bridge, the trail follows the river as it picks up speed and intensity on its rush toward the falls. The large boulders in the river were deposited here by glaciers. They represent an important chapter in the geologic story of this grand canyon that will unfold farther down the trail. Across the river on the north rim, you'll see the Canyon Bridge, built by the Army Corps of Engineers in the early days of the park. For more information on the interesting story of these historic bridges, refer to the Naturalist Notes for the North Rim of the Canyon Trail.

The rapids run faster and faster before they take a sharp turn and bound over the brink of the Upper Falls. The trail steepens, crossing several footbridges as it climbs to an overlook of this remarkable sight. For safety purposes, the National Park Service is in the process of moving the trail back from the canyon rim. The trail now detours uphill to the right around one of the wooden bridges.

Once at the overlook at Uncle Tom's parking area, you'll find the short climb was well worth the effort! From here, you have a striking view of the Upper Falls as it plunges 109 feet into the canyon. On expedition here in 1870, Nathaniel Langford wrote: *The fall...takes its leap between the jaws of rock, with a single bound into the tremendous chasm. Long before it reaches the base, it is enveloped in spray which is woven by the sun's rays into bows radiant with all colors of the prism, arching the face of the cataract with their glories.*

From this vantage point, peek through the trees on your right to look for the "third waterfall" on this trail, Crystal Falls, tucked into a fold in the other side of the canyon. After viewing these two falls, continue through the forest along the canyon rim toward the last major fall of the Yellowstone River. Soon, you come across a short spur trail to the left, known as "Uncle Tom's Trail." "Uncle" Tom Richardson was an early entreprenuer who constructed a series of stairs, ropes, and ladders scaling 500 feet down the side of the canyon in 1903. This somewhat perilous climb offered visitors spectacular views of the Lower Falls. Today, the trail is a steel staircase of 328 steps. Some people, however, still find it somewhat harrowing! If you'd like to take this steep side trip, it will add another 45 minutes to the duration of this hike. In 1889, Superintendent Frazier Boutelle received a request to install an elevator to the bottom of the canyon. The commercial exploitation of Niagara Falls inspired park managers to provide access to the features of Yellowstone in a more natural manner. Fortunately for us, Superintendent Boutelle denied this request.

From the junction with Uncle Tom's Trail, continue straight along the rim. Soon, you'll arrive at a viewing platform overlooking the canyon. If you chose not to go down Uncle Tom's Trail, this will be your first view of the magnificent 308-foot Lower Falls. You may feel something like explorer Charles Cook did in 1869 when he first came upon them:

I was riding ahead...and I remember seeing what appeared to be an opening in the forest ahead...While my attention was attracted by the pack animals...my horse suddenly stopped. I turned and looked forward from the brink of the great canyon...I sat there in amazement, while my companions came up, and after that, it seemed to me that it was five minutes before anyone spoke.

Perhaps the best way to experience these falls is, in fact, in silence. The great magnitude of this chasm is hard to grasp. It measures 20 miles long, 800 to 1,200 feet deep, and 1,500 to 4,000 feet wide. As extraordinary as its size, is its color! Naturalist John Muir noted on his visit here in 1885, *The walls of the canyon from top to bottom burn in a perfect glory of color…white, yellow, green, blue, vermilion, and various other shades of red indefinitely blending.*

Oddly enough, it's not the spectacular color of the canyon walls that gives the park its name. When fur trappers encountered Indians in what is today eastern Montana, they asked them what the name of the river was there. Apparently referring to the yellow sandstone bluffs along the river, the Indians called it "Mi tse a-da-zi" which means yellow rock or yellow stone. It's the same river, which flows through the park, that gives it its name.

Farther down the trail, you encounter another extraordinary overlook of the canyon. If you look closely, you may see steam from thermal features rising up from the bottom of the canyon. There is quite a story in this swirling steam! In a huge volcanic eruption, 640,000 years ago, ash covered thousands of square miles in a matter of minutes. Later, lava flows covered the area where you stand today. Thermal features developed within this lava flow. The heat, water, and gasses from these hot springs weakened the volcanic rock, known as rhyolite, making it more susceptible to erosion. This chemical alteration also caused iron compounds in the rock to oxidize, or rust, creating the brilliant colors that paint the canyon today. The large glacial boulders you saw when you began this hike write the next chapter in this epic geologic saga. Glaciers have filled this canyon three different times. As the most recent one began to melt, an ice dam formed upstream, holding behind it a large lake. When the dam finally broke, huge volumes of water cut through the weakened rhyolite rock, carving the canyon you see today. The rhyolite that was not hydrothermally altered did not erode away, forming the brinks of the two major falls.

From this overlook, the trail continues along the rim toward Artist Point. Before reaching it, you'll climb several switchbacks. On your travels today, maybe you've seen a white bird with black accents on its wings soaring over the canyon and diving into the river to catch fish. The osprey nests in the rugged pinnacles of the canyon walls. For a number of years, there has been an active nest in the spire below these switchbacks. Look for a circular nest, 5 to 6 feet in diameter, made of large twigs. Perhaps you'll see adult osprey feeding their young.

Not far beyond the switchbacks, you'll enter the parking area for Artist Point. The trail resumes on the far side of the parking lot. Though you'll be sharing the experience with much of America, take the short walk up the stone staircase to the upper viewing platform. Upstream is the classic view of the Lower Falls. Downriver, colors cover the canyon walls like paint on an artist's palette.

The mountain men's descriptions of this sight and the other features in Yellowstone were dismissed as tall tales. Dr. Ferdinand Hayden was sent by Congress to survey this region in 1871. Among others on the expedition, he chose to include landscape painter Thomas Moran to capture these wonders on canvas.

At what is now called Artist Point, Moran spent days trying to determine the best way to paint this grand scene. Observing the difficulty Moran was having, Dr. Hayden wrote in his journal, *Thomas Moran, who is justly celebrated for his exquisite taste as a colorist, exclaimed with a sort of regretful enthusiasm, that these beautiful tints were beyond the reach of human art.* Nonetheless, Moran persevered. In Washington, D.C., his paintings were received with great acclaim. They played an important role in convincing President Ulysses S. Grant to sign the bill establishing Yellowstone as the world's first national park. You can see Moran's massive painting of the point at which you now stand, in the Smithsonian's National Museum of American Art in Washington today. Other of his works can be seen in the Albright Visitor Center at Mammoth Hot Springs.

From here, you can either retrace your steps back along the canyon rim, or take the loop trail back to the trailhead. If you choose to continue, follow the trail that leaves from the far end of the lower viewing platform and parallels the canyon rim downstream. Here, you can enjoy the views of the canyon walls without all the people. The canyon is wild here, with no railings or fences. Watch your step. The trail steepens notably and then veers right, away from the canyon into the forest. In 0.5 mile, you reach a trail junction. Turn right and proceed 0.3 miles down a switchback, to Lily Pad Lake.

While many of Yellowstone's views are of such great magnitude it's almost difficult to take them in, this small secluded lake provides an intimate place of retreat. Only a short distance from one of the most congested places in the park, you'll have this spot all to yourself. Covered with lily pads, or "pond lilies," this little pond is appropriately named! You may see a muskrat nibbling on the long rootstalk that connects this floating flower to the lake bottom. After enjoying this pleasant place, follow the trail around the lake. You'll soon encounter the junction with the Ribbon Lake Trail, at which you turn right toward Clear Lake.

On the way to Clear Lake, you'll walk through a moonscape of mudpots, hot springs, and fumaroles. These features take on even greater significance when you understand that it was thermal features like this that led to the formation of this Grand Canyon. The trail winds through these curiosities without the benefit of a boardwalk. Keep a safe distance from these scalding features. Soon, you descend upon Clear Lake—a splash of color in this otherwise barren thermal landscape. This pretty little lake is a refreshing sight. Don't consider taking a swim, though. The waters of Clear Lake are highly acidic.

From Clear Lake, the trail begins to climb gradually through a grassland filled with wildflowers in midsummer, starting with yellow glacier lilies and pink shooting stars, and then a host of others. Make some noise here as bears also enjoy this verdant meadow. You may find them digging for the tasty roots of the glacier lily. In this grassland, you'll reach a currently unmarked trail junction. Continue straight toward the Wapiti Trailhead.

Over the crest of a small hill, the landscape changes dramatically once again. In this last mile, you'll be hiking through an open sagebrush flat on your gradual descent to the trailhead. Before long, you'll see the vast expanses of the Hayden Valley with the Yellowstone River winding through it. While Yellowstone was established as a national park primarily to protect its geothermal features, it also succeeded in preserving some of the best wildlife habitat in the lower 48 states. You may see bison here. Perhaps you've already seen many of the several thousand bison that live in the park. Never take them for granted. Bison once roamed the North American continent in numbers over 60 million strong, but after a few decades of excessive hunting, the great herds were reduced to as few as 23 individuals who survived here in Yellowstone in 1902. The bison you see are the last remnant of the great wild herds. So every time you see a bison in the park, it's a celebration—a celebration of an animal's will to survive and of the human compassion to protect them.

By now, the Wapiti Trailhead should be coming into view and your journey is complete.

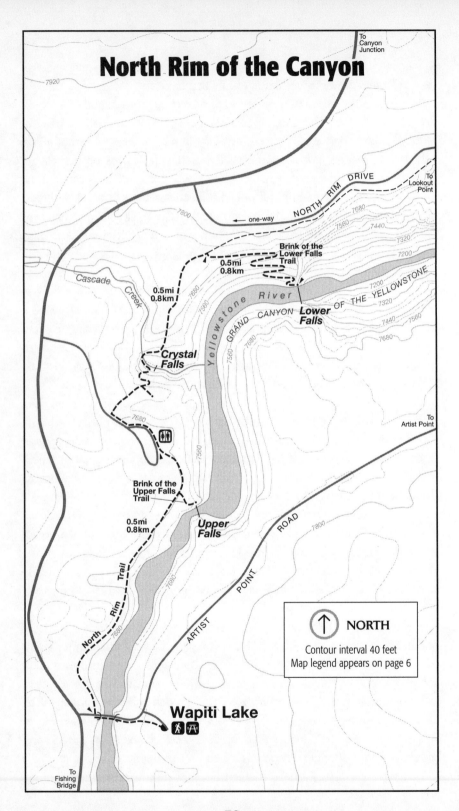

North Rim of the Canyon

To Canyon Junction

7920

NORTH RIM DRIVE

To Lookout Point

← one-way

7800

7680
7560
7440
7320
7200

Cascade Creek

Brink of the Lower Falls Trail

0.5mi
0.8km

0.5mi
0.8km

7680
7560

Yellowstone River

7200

GRAND CANYON OF THE YELLOWSTONE

7320

Lower Falls

7440
7560

7680

Crystal Falls

7680
7560

7680

To Artist Point

7680

7560

Brink of the Upper Falls Trail

0.5mi
0.8km

Upper Falls

POINT ROAD

7800

North Rim Trail

7680

ARTIST POINT

7680

↑ NORTH

Contour interval 40 feet
Map legend appears on page 6

Wapiti Lake

To Fishing Bridge

*...[the Yellowstone River] rushes eagerly, impetuously forward,
rejoicing in its strength...and goes thundering down into
the Grand Canyon in two magnificent falls.*

—Naturalist John Muir, 1885

North Rim of the Canyon

This trail takes you to the brinks of Yellowstone's two most famous waterfalls, the Upper and Lower Falls. Along the way, you'll discover the hidden "third waterfall." You'll also learn about the dramatic forces of nature that carved the Grand Canyon of the Yellowstone. *See Plate 14.*

Level of difficulty: Moderate

Distance: 3 miles round trip (4.8 km)

Elevation change: A loss of 600 feet in 0.5 mile and subsequent climb up from the brink of the Lower Falls

Duration: $1\frac{1}{2}$ - $2\frac{1}{2}$ hours

Best time of year: June through September.

Trailhead: This hike begins at the Wapiti Lake Picnic Area and Trailhead. Drive 2.3 miles south of Canyon Junction and turn left on Artist Point Road. The Wapiti Lake Picnic Area is just across the bridge on the right side of the road. The trail leaves from the picnic area. Do not take the Wapiti Lake or Howard Eaton trails on the east side of the parking area.

Hiking directions: Follow the wide paved path from the picnic area to Artist Point Road. Walk along the road's edge over the bridge to the far side. Watching for traffic, carefully cross the road. From here, the trail begins on an old road that parallels the river for about 0.5 mile before reaching the Brink of the Upper Falls. A short staircase winds down to the brink. To continue along the trail, retrace your steps back to the top of the stairs. Walk the length of the large parking lot past the restrooms for about 100 yards. Beyond this parking area along the roadside, you'll see the trail to your right and the sign that marks the "North Rim Trail." Soon the trail meets the canyon. To your right, a path leads to an overlook of Crystal Falls. After viewing the falls, continue back along the main trail, crossing Cascade Creek. Twisting and turning, the trail passes through a boggy wetland before emerging onto a series of switchbacks leading down to the brink of the Lower Falls. To return, retrace your steps back to the trailhead.

Special attention: The canyon walls are steep and unforgiving. Keep your distance from the rims. The waterfalls plunge steeply over the brinks. Stay behind the railings.

Naturalist notes: You can drive to access points for each of the falls, but this short walk allows you to witness the change in the Yellowstone River and anticipate the energy of the rushing waters before they plunge into the canyon.

Once you've walked over the bridge and crossed the road to where the trail begins, you've begun a walk back in time. The first bridge to span this 120 foot chasm of the canyon was constructed in 1903 under the command of Captain Hiram Chittenden. The Army built many of the early roads and bridges in the park and they were known for their fine craftsmanship. By the 1960s, frost and weathering had taken their toll on the bridge. Unfortunately, it had also proven too narrow for modern vehicles. In 1962, it was replaced by the present day bridge, which retains the historic character of the original. Named the Chittenden Memorial Bridge, it honors the captain's notable contribution toward making many major features accessible to park visitors.

You may be disappointed that the North Rim Trail is actually an old road. Don't be. This is part of the historic journey. As the original stagecoach route, it escorted early visitors to the grand views of the falls. Today, it will do the same for you. The Yellowstone River below you is also on a journey, cutting back and forth on its way to the brink. Notice its increasing speed and urgency as you venture together downstream.

Before long, you cross another historic bridge, the Canyon Bridge, which was built in the late 1890s. You can imagine the stagecoach stopping here, to let the women with their parasols and the men in their dusters admire the large boulders in the river with the trees growing out of them, the rapids getting larger and wilder, and the river rushing faster on its race to the brink. Soon you reach a stone stairway that takes you down to the Upper Falls.

Hold on to the railings. Watching water fall 109 feet can be a dizzying experience! The canyon walls suddenly narrow, forcing this wide river into a raging torrent. Banking hard to the right, it gains speed and intensity and then leaps off the brink as if unaware of the precipice beneath it. The water strikes the bottom of the canyon with such force that it rebounds up in columns of water looking like geysers erupting from the river below.

The noted naturalist, John Muir wrote of this place:

For the first 20 miles [the river's] course is a level, sunny valley…through which it flows in silvery reaches…making no sound save a low whispering among the sedges. Then suddenly, as if preparing for hard work, it rushes eagerly, impetuously forward rejoicing in its strength…and goes thundering down into the Grand Canon in two magnificent falls, one hundred and three hundred feet high.

Back up the stairs and en route to the Lower Falls, you'll have a brush with civilization as you walk alongside the parking area. A few hundred yards down the road, the trail turns right into the forest. When you reach the rim, a path to the right brings you to an encounter with the "third waterfall" as it's known to some local rangers. Though it's just yards away from the parking lot, most people will miss this remarkable, well hidden waterfall, which is tucked into a fold in the canyon. Crystal Falls is what happens to Cascade Creek as it drops 129 feet over the canyon wall. Continue along the North Rim Trail as it winds above the falls, providing several intriguing views of Cascade Creek. The trail then parallels the rim and passes through a small meadow before placing you on the first of 9 switchbacks on your 600 foot descent to the brink of the Lower Falls.

On the way down, try to imagine water falling three times as far as what you observed earlier at the Upper Falls. The view of the brink will take your breath away. If heights bother you, it may also make you weak in the knees. The energy exerted in this 309 foot fall can be overwhelming. The river falls over the brink with enormous power and equal grace. The sun catches the spray of the thundering water and refracts it into a beautiful rainbow. This must be among the most inspiring sights that Yellowstone has to offer.

At the brink, you get not only views of the waterfall, but also of the exquisite canyon it adorns. As you steady yourself, consider the awesome forces of nature that carved this incomparable canyon. Here your journey takes a leap from the confines of human history to the magnitudes of geologic time.

This stunning display of nature's handiwork began when the last volcanic eruptions laid down lava flows in the area. Later, a geyser basin formed within the lava flow. You can still see thermal activity in the canyon today. The hot water, steam, and gasses of these geysers and hot springs hydrothermally altered the normally hard lava, known as rhyolite, weakening the rock and making it susceptible to erosion and further downcutting by the river. At the edges of these thermal basins, however, the hard, resistant, unaltered lavas remained to form the brinks of the two falls.

Later, it's believed that glaciers assisted in the sculpting of the canyon, but not by the brute force of ice. Rather, the glaciers created ice dams near Yellowstone Lake that held ice and water. As the ice began to melt, the dams eventually gave way, releasing a deluge downstream. This huge volume of water flowing through the soft rock further eroded and defined the present appearance of the canyon. Nowhere else have the combined powers of fire and ice come together to create so sublime a work of nature as the Grand Canyon of the Yellowstone.

If you're interested in more information on the Canyon, refer to the Naturalist Notes of the South Rim of the Canyon Trail.

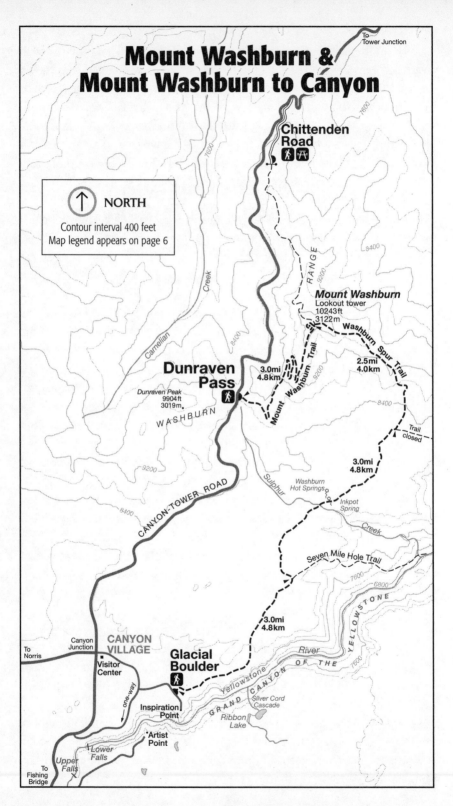

Mount Washburn &
Mount Washburn to Canyon

To Tower Junction

Chittenden Road

NORTH

Contour interval 400 feet
Map legend appears on page 6

RANGE

8400

9200

8600

Mount Washburn
Lookout tower
10243ft
3122m

Washburn Spur Trail

Creek

Carnelian

8400

Dunraven Pass

3.0mi
4.8km

2.5mi
4.0km

Mount Washburn Trail

9200

Dunraven Peak
9904ft
3019m

WASHBURN

8400

Trail closed

9200

Sulphur

Washburn Hot Springs

3.0mi
4.8km

CANYON-TOWER ROAD

8400

Inkpot Spring

Creek

Seven Mile Hole Trail

7600

6800

YELLOWSTONE

3.0mi
4.8km

Canyon Junction

CANYON VILLAGE

To Norris

Visitor Center

River

Glacial Boulder

GRAND CANYON OF THE

7600

one-way

Inspiration Point

Silver Cord Cascade

Ribbon Lake

Artist Point

Yellowstone

Lower Falls

Upper Falls

To Fishing Bridge

If I could only choose one sight, in the wonderland, it would be,
by all means, that view from the top of Mount Washburn for you see
there the entire park spread out before you in a single picture.
—Park visitor Colgate Hunt, 1878

Mount Washburn &
Mount Washburn to Canyon

It's the conventional wisdom among many rangers that if you can hike only one trail in Yellowstone, it should be Mount Washburn. The trail up this ancient peak passes through one of the best collections of wildflowers in the park. At the summit, much of Yellowstone's finest scenery is displayed in sweeping panoramic views. Watch for the elusive Rocky Mountain bighorn sheep who make these mountains their summer home. *See Plate 15.*

Mount Washburn

Level of difficulty: Strenuous

Distance: 6 miles round trip (9.6 km)

Elevation change: A gain of 1,400 feet in 3 miles

Duration: 3 - 4 hours

Mount Washburn to Canyon

Level of difficulty: Strenuous

Distance: 11.5 miles (18.4 km) one way. *This hike requires a shuttle back to the trailhead.*

Elevation change: A gain of 1,400 feet in 3 miles and a loss of 2,000 feet in 2.5 miles

Duration: 6 - 8 hours

Best time of year: Mid-July through September. Snow drifts can cover much of the trail during the first part of the summer. Late July and early August are optimal for wildflowers.

Trailhead: This hike begins in the parking area for the Dunraven Pass Trailhead on the east side of the road, 5 miles (8 km) north of Canyon Junction. Do not confuse this with the Dunraven Road Picnic Area, farther south.

Hiking directions: From the trailhead, begin the steady climb to the top of the mountain. Just before the summit, the trail comes to a large junction at a hair-pin turn in the Chittenden Road Trail that joins this trail from the north. Veer left and continue the short distance to the lookout tower. To return to the trail-head, retrace your steps to Dunraven Pass.

For those continuing on to Canyon, as the trail leaves the summit, it will soon meet the Washburn Spur Trail at the wide hairpin turn junction. Take the Washburn Spur Trail to the left (east) through the tundra. This trail is level for a short distance. Then, it descends very steeply off the southeast slope of Mount Washburn, losing 2,000 feet in 2.5 miles without the aid of switchbacks. The trail levels at the junction with the Howard Eaton Trail. To your left, the trail is permanently closed as part of a bear management area. Veer to the right and continue for 3 miles through forests, large meadows, and the Washburn Hot Springs to reach the junction with the Seven Mile Hole Trail. Turn right and hike another 3 miles past a view of Silver Cord Cascade across the canyon. Continue to the Glacial Boulder Trailhead near Inspiration Point.

Special attention: Grizzly bears frequent this trail throughout the season, par-ticularly on the Spur Trail between Mount Washburn and Canyon. Be alert and make noise if at any time you can't see clearly in all directions. The summit of Mount Washburn can be cold and windy even on nice days. Be prepared for quickly changing weather conditions by bringing along some warm clothing and wind- and raingear. The trail down the Washburn Spur is extremely steep in places. Wear good hiking boots for traction and watch your footing on loose rocks. In recent years, finding a place to park at the Dunraven Pass Trailhead has been difficult. An alternative trailhead is Chittenden Road, which is located about 5 miles north of the Dunraven Pass Trailhead. Here, you'll find plenty of parking, and the hiking distance and elevation gain are the same.

Naturalist notes: The trip up Mount Washburn is a journey back in geologic time. You'll be hiking to the top of an ancient volcano that erupted some 50 million years ago when many of the Rocky Mountains were being formed. As you climb the 1,400 feet up this volcanic remnant, you'll notice the terrain is composed mostly of breccia, angular chunks of rock embedded in volcanic ash.

The trail follows the remains of a wagon road constructed in 1905. Imagine stagecoaches ferrying people to the top of this mountain. In the 1920s, Model T Fords also made the climb, but in reverse, since this was the only means of getting fuel to the engine! Today, this wide trail winds its way to high elevations amid the same grand scenery these early travelers enjoyed.

One of the first things you'll notice as you depart the trailhead is the broad green slopes filled with wildflowers adorning the meadows and valleys below. From late July to early August, the slopes of Mount Washburn display one of the loveliest arrays of wildflowers anywhere in the park. Color abounds in flow-ers—mountain sunflowers, Indian paintbrush, bluebells, lupine, phlox, fireweed, cow parsnip, geraniums, and shooting stars, to name but a few.

Midway through the 3-mile climb up Mount Washburn, the trail begins to switchback. Occasionally, you'll get a glimpse of the lookout tower above you, awaiting your arrival at the summit. With each new turn in the trail, the views get finer. It was for views like these that the mountain originally got its name. In 1870, an exploring party from Montana known as the Washburn Expedition ventured into the Yellowstone region prior to its establishment as a national park. As days passed and fears mounted of Indian attacks and of losing their way, the group's leader, General Henry D. Washburn, elected to ascend the peak, hoping to map the view and secure a route through the Yellowstone wilderness. The words from the journal of Nathaniel Langford, a member of the expedition who went on to become the park's first superintendent, described the moment best:

General Washburn rode out to make a reconnaissance…and returned…with the intelligence that from the summit of a high mountain he had seen Yellowstone Lake, the proposed object of our visit. This…has greatly relieved our anxiety concerning the course we are to pursue, and has quieted the dread apprehensions of some of our num-ber…we have spontaneously and by unanimous vote given the mountain the name by which it will hereafter and forever be known, "Mount Washburn."

Farther along the trail, you'll encounter stands of whitebark pine, Engelmann spruce, and subalpine fir, typical of higher elevations. Since few day hikes in Yellowstone reach the heights where such forests grow, enjoy these trees as you climb the mountain. Take note, too, of what happens to these same species near timberline at 10,000 feet. The once large and healthy looking whitebark pine becomes a twisted, stunted, dwarfed image of its former self, taking on an almost "bonsai" appearance. Harsh weather has sculpted these trees into their current form. Wind and cold have scoured them to the point that little growth occurs on the trees' windward sides. The trees bend to the will of the wind.

Nearing the top, you'll follow the spine of a narrow ridge as you enter the world of subalpine tundra. Here, where the weather is so severe, life clings to the earth to avoid the continuous drying winds of this inhospitable environ-ment. One of the most popular and beloved flowers here is the tiny alpine for-get-me-not. Distinctively bright blue with yellow centers, they bloom where most plants won't even grow. Despite their ability to adapt, alpine flowers are very sensitive. With such a short growing season these delicate tundra plants need our help if they are to endure. Please stay on the designated trails. Even treading lightly off-trail can irreparably harm this most fragile ecosystem.

As you're hiking, keep an eye out for the elusive Rocky Mountain bighorn sheep. The rocky outcrops of Mount Washburn provide the perfect summer retreat for these sure-footed creatures of the high country, renowned for the fully curled horn of the mature adult ram. The rams, however, are seldom seen here. You're more likely to see the females and their young. If you're going to see a bighorn in Yellowstone, this is one of the best places to do so. They blend in well with their surroundings and can often be found among the craggiest precipices, evading predators and sometimes the searching human eye.

Just below the summit, the trail meets the Chittenden Road Trail coming in from the north. Also, to the right at this wide intersection, is the Washburn Spur Trail, leading toward Canyon. Wind your way the short distance to the top of the mountain. At the summit, you'll want to get out of the wind and cold by going into a small observation room beneath the lookout tower. Inside this proverbial glass house, you'll find a high power telescope to aid you in the search for wildlife and in enjoying the grand scenery. In the big meadows below, look for elk and grizzly bears. You'll also find a record book where people have entered their impressions of this experience. Take a moment to record your own thoughts. From the observation room and the outdoor deck upstairs, you are afforded some of the most magnificent views in Yellowstone. On a trip to the park in the summer of 1875, General William Emerson Strong captured the essence of this mountain when he wrote:

Tired and breathless we gained the summit of Mount Washburn, and in an instant of time, without the faintest warning, the whole grand panorama burst upon us. At our feet, as it were, lay spread out for our inspection the mysterious country we have come so far to see…Wonderland. Grand, glorious, and magnificent was the scene as we looked upon it…No pen can write it—no language describe it.

Indeed, from this lofty height of 10,243 feet, the view does take in much of the park, which is truly hard to describe. Before you, to the east and south, is the Grand Canyon of the Yellowstone and, beyond it, Hayden Valley and Yellowstone Lake. To the west are the Gallatins, to the east the Absarokas creating the park boundary, and to the south, the Grand Tetons appear in the far distance. When it's cold, steam can be seen rising from the geyser basins at Norris and Old Faithful.

The power of the Yellowstone landscape makes it a difficult place to leave. When you decide to descend from this mountaintop experience, retrace your route down to the Dunraven Pass Trailhead.

If you still have the time, energy and endurance, consider hiking the Washburn Spur Trail to Canyon. Just below the summit at the large intersection at the hairpin turn, you'll see the trail sign and path taking off to the east. This is the Spur Trail. It follows along a flank of the volcano through rocky terrain and more dwarfed and gnarled whitebark pine and spruce. After climbing up a little knob, the trail begins a serious descent, dropping 2,000 feet in 2.5 miles without the aid of switchbacks. Be very careful. The trail is quite steep as it descends the southeast flank of the mountain. The views are simply incredible, with Mount Washburn above and the Grand Canyon of the Yellowstone below. Past the canyon lie the glistening waters of Yellowstone Lake and beyond it, the Red Mountains and the Tetons.

As you lose elevation, you'll begin to pass through large mature stands of whitebark pine mixed with more big spruce and fir. In 2.5 miles, the trail levels off at the intersection with the Howard Eaton Trail. To the left, the trail is closed. A metal sign announces that the trail beyond is within a permanently closed bear management area. Such closures have been put into effect by the National Park Service as a means of helping the threatened grizzly bear recover in the Greater Yellowstone Ecosystem. At the trail junction, veer right and continue hiking through what can be best described as an enchanted landscape of big trees and grassy meadows strewn with wildflowers and mossy stream crossings. This forest definitely gets your attention. Real or imagined, you get the clear sense that there are bears in these woods. You're hiking in grizzly bear country now, so make your presence known with plenty of noise.

After crossing a large meadow from which there's a clear view of Mount Washburn, the trail reenters the forest and encounters the surreal setting of the Washburn Hot Springs. Yellow sulfur deposits color the barren thermal earth. The smell of sulfur thickens the air. Hot springs and mudpots filled with iron sulfide bubble and churn. Here, you get a feel for the primeval nature of Mother Earth. You may wonder what lurks at greater depths. The presence of thermal activity serves as a reminder that you've entered the 640,000 year old Yellowstone caldera, resulting from one of the largest volcanic events in earth's history.

Just past the springs, the trail crosses Sulphur Creek. Look for a log to aid you across. Continue hiking in and out of small thermal areas until you reach the junction with the Seven Mile Hole Trail. Turn right, and pass through a forest that, at an elevation close to 8,000 feet, is mostly lodgepole pine. Somewhere out there lies the Grand Canyon of the Yellowstone, but this dense forest hides it well. It's easy to see how these forests made it difficult for early explorers to find such treasures.

In about 2 miles, the trees begin to recede and the north rim of the canyon appears on the left. Across the canyon, you'll be afforded a fine view of Silver Cord Cascade as it tumbles 800 feet over the south rim into the canyon. From here, the trail parallels the canyon, which comes in and out of view for the final mile. You'll emerge at the Glacial Boulder Trailhead near Inspiration Point. Hopefully, this experience will have been inspirational for you.

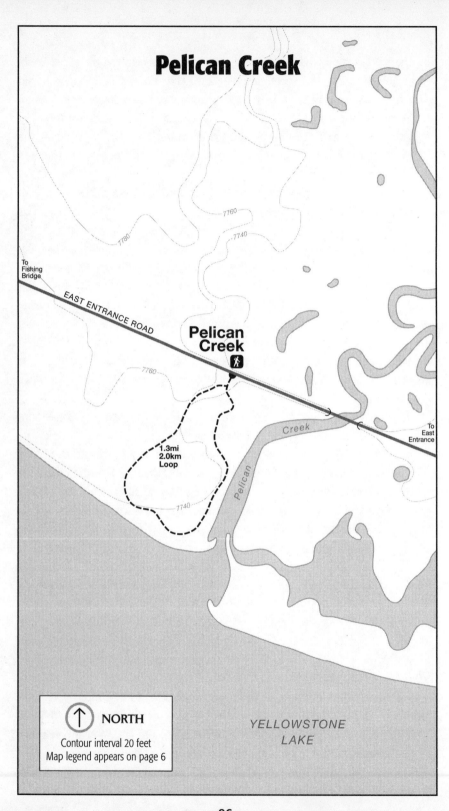

Pelican Creek

7760
7740
7780

To
Fishing
Bridge

EAST ENTRANCE ROAD

Pelican
Creek

7760

1.3mi
2.0km
Loop

7740

Creek

Pelican

To
East
Entrance

↑ NORTH

Contour interval 20 feet
Map legend appears on page 6

YELLOWSTONE
LAKE

Pelican Creek

It's hard to believe that Nature could put so much into one mile. This short trail passes through the forest, along the shore of Yellowstone Lake, and among the rich wetlands of Pelican Creek in an easy loop. Often, the pelicans for whom the trail is named can be seen at the mouth of the creek. Birders favor this trail since the diversity of habitat is home to many other bird species, as well. *See Plate 16.*

Level of difficulty: Easy

Distance: 1.3-mile loop (2 km)

Elevation change: Minimal

Duration: 30 minutes - 1 hour

Best time of year: Late June through September. In spring, grizzly bears travel along the lakeshore to find cutthroat trout in the spawning streams around the lake. Inquire at the Fishing Bridge Visitor Center for recent bear sightings in the area before hiking this trail in spring.

Trailhead: This hike begins at the pullout 1 mile (1.6 km) east of Fishing Bridge on the south side of the East Entrance Road.

Hiking directions: Take the trail on the right side of the loop as it winds through the forest for about 0.5 mile, where it meets Yellowstone Lake. The trail parallels the lakeshore and then crosses the marsh on a boardwalk that leads back to the trailhead.

Special attention: The high waters of Pelican Creek can flood the boardwalk through the marsh in spring.

Naturalist notes: Following the path to the right, you're immediately immersed in a lodgepole pine forest. This is an old lodgepole forest that is giving way to the climax forest of spruces and firs. You'll notice the young trees reaching up to the sun. Enjoy the sights and sounds of the woodland, because very soon the trail brings you to an entirely different habitat, the lakeshore.

Although the trail doesn't go down to the lake, you should. Take some time to enjoy the grand views of Yellowstone Lake. The beach is perfect for a little introspection. Don't wander too far however, as this stretch of lakeshore is home to several sensitive plants and birds that shouldn't be disturbed. Watch closely for bald eagles or osprey fishing. The osprey, which can dive underwater, is the better fisher of the two. The eagle can only snatch a fish from the surface, so it's likely to try to steal one from the osprey! Canada geese, mallards, and Barrow's goldeneyes are residents here. Not so common are the common loons, who inhabit the lake in spring and fall. Like the elk, their distinctive call is a familiar sound on crisp autumn mornings. The magnificent trumpeter swans are also visitors to the lake in fall.

But the local hero is the American white pelican. You may see a flock gathering on the sandbar at the mouth of Pelican Creek. Unlike their cousins, the brown pelicans, who are renowned divers, these birds float together in a circle to fish for the cutthroat trout. They bob up and down in unison until suddenly as if on cue, all submerge at once, bringing up their catch in their huge bills. They can hold several trout in their pouch at once and five times as much in their bill as in their stomach! Poet Ogden Nash was inspired to pen the whimsical rhyme, *A strange bird is the pelican. His beak can hold more than his belly can.* Pelicans are incredibly effective fishers and may pull more fish out of Yellowstone Lake than their human counterparts. In the early part of the century, this nearly led to this big white bird's demise.

In the 1920s, fishermen complained that they weren't catching as many fish as they had in previous years. Even though millions of trout were being harvested and hundreds of millions of eggs were being taken from Yellowstone's fish hatcheries, park managers laid the blame for the decline in fishing at the webbed feet of the white pelican. It was also alleged that pelicans were passing on a parasite to cutthroat trout. For three terrible years, park biologists went out to the pelican nesting site on the Molly Islands in the Southeast Arm of Yellowstone Lake and crushed hundreds of eggs. It was a low point in our understanding of what national parks were intended to preserve. Now, a balance is sought between providing recreational experiences for people and preserving native species. In fact, when there is any doubt, the animals win. Today, the pelican is as protected as any other species in Yellowstone. Enjoy these symbolic and charismatic critters while you can. When a chill comes to the air in fall, they'll be gone until next spring, wintering as far south as the Yucatan Peninsula.

The pelican is not the only creature who takes advantage of the cutthroat trout here. Grizzly bears have also discovered this windfall of food in spring, hence the caution to avoid this trail at that time. Before blending its waters into the lake, Pelican Creek winds through Pelican Valley, some of the richest grizzly bear habitat in the lower 48 states.

Back on the trail, you'll get a good look at the creek as it ends its journey in a wide meander at the lake. From the boardwalk, you'll experience the incredibly lush green wetland Pelican Creek creates. It's worth spending some time with the view across the marsh to the lake and the mountains beyond. The abundance of aquatic plants here occasionally attracts moose to these wetlands. Birders will be hoping to catch a glimpse of the elusive sora, a wading bird or rail, whose camouflaged coloring and secretive ways make it a rare find indeed. If you're really lucky, you may see a snipe among the water plants of the marsh.

Before long, the boardwalk leads back to the trailhead and your brief sojourn at Pelican Creek is complete.

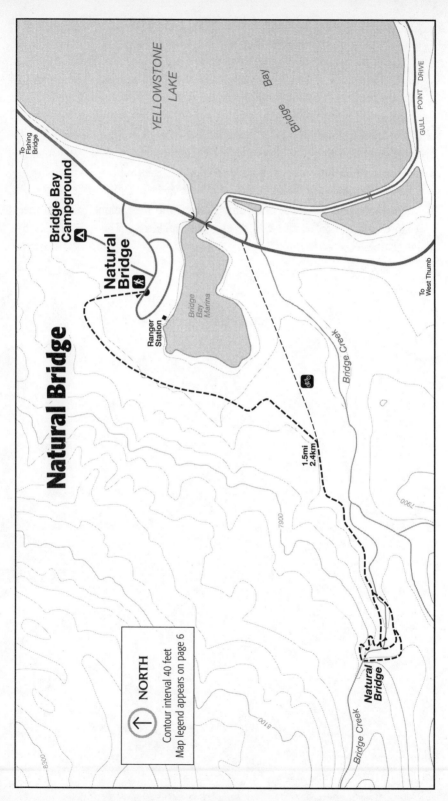

Natural Bridge

NORTH

Contour interval 40 feet
Map legend appears on page 6

YELLOWSTONE
LAKE

Bridge
Bay

GULL POINT DRIVE

To
Fishing
Bridge

Bridge Bay
Campground

Natural
Bridge

Bridge
Bay
Marina

Ranger
Station

To
West Thumb

Bridge Creek

1.5mi
2.4km

7900

8100

7900

8100

8300

8500

Bridge Creek

Natural
Bridge

We found a most singular natural bridge which gives passing to a small stream.

—Explorer Dr. Ferdinand Hayden, 1871

Natural Bridge

Most people associate natural arches and bridges with the national parks of the southwest. Few are aware of the one here in Yellowstone. This leisurely stroll takes you through the forest and alongside a meadow to Yellowstone's own natural bridge. *See Plate 17.*

Level of difficulty: Easy

Distance: 3 miles round trip (4.8 km)

Elevation change: An optional 50 foot elevation gain in a few hundred yards to the top of the natural bridge.

Duration: 1 - 2 hours

Best time of year: Late June through September. This trail is not open in spring due to an annual bear management closure. During this time, grizzly bears have been known to feed on the cutthroat trout spawning in Bridge Creek. Park rangers will open this trail in mid- to late June when the spawn is over. Inquire at the Bridge Bay Ranger Station or the Fishing Bridge Visitor Center for the opening date.

Trailhead: This hike begins at the Bridge Bay Marina parking area, near the extended use parking lot for boat trailers. Do not confuse this trailhead with that of the bike path, which is a paved road located just south of the marina on the main road.

Hiking directions: The trail begins across the road from the Bridge Bay Marina parking area. Follow the paved path that parallels the entrance road to the campground. Upon reaching the campsites, the trail takes a sharp left turn. It continues through the forest for about 0.5 mile before reaching the junction with the old road that is currently a bike path. The road then winds alongside a long narrow meadow on the way to the natural bridge. A short switchback trail leads to the top of the bridge. It then crosses the creek behind the bridge and loops back to the road.

Naturalist notes: Past the campground, the trail crosses three wooden footbridges over small wetlands before it meets the bike path. This section of trail goes through a shady forest. Here, you'll witness the natural succession of a lodgepole pine forest. Old trees reach to the sky creating a dense canopy, while young lodgepole pines, Engelmann spruces, and subalpine firs sprout up in the few patches of sunlight available. A changing cast of wildflowers adorns the forest floor as the season progresses. Several unofficial trails lead down to the marina. Stay on the main trail to the bridge.

The trail parallels the shore of Bridge Bay. A member of one of the early exploring parties, David Folsom, wrote of this bay, *This was one of the beautiful places we had found fashioned by the practised hand of nature, that man had not desecrated.* These words may seem a bit ironic in light of how developed the area has become in recent times. Bridge Bay is a natural bay. After World War II, the National Park Service undertook an effort to build more recreational facilities to accommodate the postwar increase in visitors to the parks. In this era, Bridge Bay was dredged out to create the marina. Current park philosophy leans more toward careful preservation of natural features such as this.

About halfway down the trail, four large boulders appear across your path. These are not intended to keep you off the rest of the trail, but to keep bicycles from going on the footpath. This is the junction with the bicycle trail. Veer right.

Many of the park's first roads were originally built by the Army in the early days of the park to make interesting features accessible to visitors. This one was once part of the original stagecoach road from West Thumb to Lake. Visitors could drive to the natural bridge until 1991, when it was closed to make more opportunities for people to bicycle in Yellowstone, since hiking trails are not open to bicycles in the park.

The road curves gently alongside a long narrow meadow through which Bridge Creek runs. As you get nearer to the natural bridge, this small creek becomes more visible. Bridge Creek is a spawning creek for cutthroat trout. It's the type of creek that grizzly bears favor the most. The creek is narrow and shallow, and fish remain relatively still while they spawn, making it easy for bears to stand in the creek and fish. This trail is closed during the trout spawn so hikers won't have a close encounter with a hungry bear.

Just before the natural bridge, the road makes a large loop. The most direct route is to the right. At the top of the loop, the bridge comes into view. Dr. Ferdinand Hayden is credited with discovering this intriguing feature on expedition here with the U.S. Geological Survey in 1871. His description of it as "a most singular natural bridge" is appropriate since it's the only one of its kind in Yellowstone. Though Dr. Hayden's discovery of this bridge is noteworthy, it's likely that any number of native American people had found it prior to him.

Near the bridge, an historic wayside exhibit will inform you that the natural bridge is 51 feet high and spans 29 feet across the creek. To determine how the bridge was created, follow the short switchback trail to the top. Along the way you'll see the creek as it falls 10 feet over a rock face under the natural bridge. You might wonder how this tiny creek, almost non-existent in fall, could have carved this massive bridge.

It had some help from the harsh temperatures of winter in these high mountains. The rock that comprises the bridge is the vertical edge of a lava flow from an eruption 140,000 years ago. Water from the creek found its way into the cracks in the rock. As the water froze, it expanded, breaking off pieces of rock that were later carried away by wind and water, leaving the bridge arching overhead. The natural bridge is a testament to the power of water and ice.

In a few switchbacks, you reach the top of the bridge. Enjoy the view of the lake from above, but do not cross the bridge. It is a fragile geological feature as well as a human safety hazard! Near the top of the bridge, the trail turns right and enters a steep ravine.

Once in the ravine, you find yourself looking down through the hole that Bridge Creek carved to form this unusual bridge. A spruce tree grows in the center of the bridge. It's amazing that such a tree could grow with so little soil on this hard rock face. One also has to wonder if another type of erosion, roots versus rock, might eventually crack the bridge in two.

The trail continues out of the ravine and along the rim of the cliff before rejoining the road. In the early days of the park, the second Superintendent, Philetus Norris, constructed a horse trail across the bridge and proposed building a stagecoach road over it, as well. Fortunately for us, this never occurred, so the bridge is still intact for us to enjoy today.

To return, follow the road around the loop for some nice views looking back at the natural bridge before returning by the same route to the trailhead.

Water never seemed so beautiful before.
—Explorer Nathaniel Langford, 1870

18

Storm Point

This trail is one of the most scenic short hikes in Yellowstone. Starting in the pastoral setting of Indian Pond, the trail leads to a bluff overlooking the vast expanses of Yellowstone Lake. It then follows the shoreline through the forest before reaching Storm Point. This rocky point affords more striking views of Yellowstone Lake and the mountain ranges that surround it. *See Plate 18.*

Level of difficulty: Easy

Distance: 2.3-mile loop (3.7 km)

Elevation change: Minimal

Duration: 1 - 2 hours

Best time of year: Late June through September. In spring, the lakeshore becomes a corridor for grizzly bears traveling between cutthroat trout spawning streams. Inquire at the Fishing Bridge Visitor Center about recent bear sightings in the area before hiking this trail.

Trailhead: This hike begins at Indian Pond, 2.7 miles (4.6 km) east of Fishing Bridge on the East Entrance Road.

Hiking directions: The trail begins by paralleling the west shore of Indian Pond. After several hundred yards, it passes a trail that leads off to the right, which is the return loop. Bypass this trail and continue straight out to the bluffs overlooking Yellowstone Lake. From here, the trail bends to the right and follows along the bluff until it crosses a small footbridge. Across the bridge, it turns sharply to the left, passing through the forest until opening up into a meadow before Storm Point. A short spur trail leads out to the point itself. To continue on the loop trail, retrace your steps off the point and proceed west on the sandy bluffs above the lake. Soon, the trail turns away from the lake and enters the forest. In the forest, the trail loops back for about 0.5 mile before reaching the sagebrush flats, Indian Pond, and the return to the trailhead.

Special attention: Be aware of bison who often graze near the pond. Remember to stay at least 25 yards away from all wildlife and 100 yards from bears.

Storm Point

Storm Point

To East Entrance

EAST ENTRANCE ROAD

To Fishing Bridge

Indian Pond

2.3mi
3.7km
Loop

Mary

Bay

↑ NORTH

Contour interval 20 feet
Map legend appears on page 6

Storm Point

YELLOWSTONE LAKE

Naturalist notes: Standing at the trailhead, you are treated to one of the finest views in Yellowstone. The sparkling gem of Indian Pond is set against the backdrop of Yellowstone Lake, framed by the Absaroka Range.

The tranquil waters of this small pond offer little evidence of its explosive past. According to one theory, Indian Pond erupted onto the landscape much as a geyser would. A thermal area was once held under pressure here beneath a massive glacier. As the climate warmed and the ice melted and began to recede, the pressure was released and the pond erupted suddenly into existence. Other scientists, however, disagree with this view. They believe that silica-laden waters, rising up through sandy sediments, glued these sediments together to form a hard cap over the hydrothermal basin. Heat and pressure, building up below, eventually exploded away the cap rocks, leaving this spectacular circle of deep water.

Indian Pond is named for the fact that several tribes were known to camp here, perhaps even Chief Joseph and the Nez Perce as they fled from the Army through Yellowstone in 1877 on their ill-fated flight to freedom in Canada.

Beyond the pond, the trail passes through a meadow of wildflowers frequented by bison. If you don't see bison, you may see signs of their presence. Look for wallows, the circular depressions where bison have worn away the grass as they roll on the ground to shed their winter coats and fend off insects. Nearby, many of the lodgepole pines have been stripped of their bark where they, too, have been rubbed by bison.

Soon the trail arrives at a bluff overlooking Yellowstone Lake. It's easy to understand why early explorers referred to the lake as a "vast inland sea." It's the largest lake at high elevation in North America, measuring 20 miles long and 14 miles wide, with 110 miles of shoreline. A hydrothermal explosion, much like the one that may have formed Indian Pond, also created Mary Bay, to the east. This geothermal activity in the lake is not just a thing of the past.

In the last decade, the U.S. Geological Survey and the University of Wisconsin's Center for Great Lakes Studies have done research here that has revolutionized our understanding of Yellowstone Lake. A remotely operated submarine, similar to the one used to examine the shipwreck of the *Titanic,* explored the bottom of the lake, videotaping all it encountered. After these journeys, researchers concluded that if you could figuratively pour all the water out of Yellowstone Lake, what you'd find on the bottom is something very similar to what you find on land—geysers, hot springs, and deep canyons! If the lake is calm, you might just see thermal waters bubbling up next to Storm Point. Until recently, maps of the lake suggested that its deepest point was 320 feet. Based on these studies, we now know that one of the deepest canyons in the lake is just east off Stevenson Island, reaching a depth of 390 feet or more. They've also discovered rock spires of hydrothermal origin rising 90 feet from the lake bottom. Yellowstone was established as the world's first national park in 1872 primarily because of its "geothermal curiosities." Who would have ever thought that some of the greatest wonders of all are only now, over 125 years later, beginning to be discovered?

Crossing a creek on a footbridge, the trail winds through a spruce-fir forest until it opens up into a strikingly different landscape. As you walk past sand dunes of earlier lakeshores, the first dramatic view of Storm Point comes into sight. On the way to the rocky point, listen for a high pitched chirping sound. Step quietly here. The large boulders ahead are home to a colony of yellow-bellied marmots. They may be basking in the sun, rolling over to greet you with a bemused stare. These curious creatures live the good life. They spend the summer enjoying the sunshine and then sleep the winter away in hibernation.

Take the short trail out to Storm Point and enjoy the grand view. The

Plate 1. Narrow Gauge Terrace Trail, Mammoth Area (See page 14)

Plate 2. Beaver Ponds Trail, Mammoth Area (See page 18)

Plate 3. The Hoodoos Trail, Mammoth Area (See page 23)

Plate 4. Bunsen Peak Trail, Mammoth Area (See page 28)

Plate 5. Yellowstone River Picnic Area Trail, Tower Area (See page 34)

Plate 6. Lost Lake and Petrified Tree Loop Trail, Tower Area (See page 38)

Plate 7. Slough Creek Trail, Tower Area (See page 43)

Plate 8. Yellowstone River on the Hellroaring Creek Trail, Tower Area (See page 47)

Plate 9. The Petrified Trees Trail, Tower Area (See page 52)

Plate 10. Trout Lake Trail, Lamar Valley Area (See page 56)

Plate 11. Pebble Creek Trail, Lamar Valley Area (See page 60)

Plate 12. Cascade Lake/Observation Peak Trail, Canyon Area (See page 65)

Plate 13. Artist Point, South Rim of the Canyon Trail (See page 70)

Plate 14. Brink of the Lower Falls, North Rim of the Canyon Trail (See page 76)

Plate 15. Mount Washburn Trail, Canyon Area (See page 80)

Plate 16. Pelican Creek Trail, Lake Area (See page 86)

Plate 17. Natural Bridge Trail, Lake Area (See page 90)

Plate 18. Storm Point Trail, Lake Area (See page 94)

Plate 19. Elephant Back Mountain Trail, Lake Area (See page 98)

Plate 20. Avalanche Peak Trail, Lake Area (See page 102)

Plate 21. Lake Overlook Trail, Grant Area (See page 107)

Plate 22. Riddle Lake Trail, Grant Area (See page 111)

Plate 23. Shoshone Lake Trail, Grant Area (See page 116)

Plate 24. Observation Point Trail, Old Faithful Area (See page 120)

Plate 25. Lone Star Geyser Trail, Old Faithful Area (See page 125)

Plate 26. Mystic Falls and Overlook Trail, Old Faithful Area (See page 129)

Plate 27. Imperial Geyser on the Fairy Falls Trail, Old Faithful Area (See page 134)

Plate 28. Artists' Paintpots Trail, Madison/Norris Area (See page 140)

Plate 29. Monument Geyser Basin (See page 145)

Absaroka Range rises to the east, the Red Mountains to the south, and the Grand Tetons in between. True to its name, this point is often battered by storms. On expedition here in 1870 explorer, Nathaniel Langford wrote of the changing weather and changing moods of Yellowstone Lake:

Yesterday it lay before us calm and unruffled, save the waves which gently broke upon the shore. Today, the winds lash it into a raging sea, covering its surface with foam, while sparkling sand along the shore seems to form for it a jeweled setting. Water never seemed so beautiful before.

Perhaps one of the most important values that the national parks preserve is one of the simplest—beauty. The parks were created, first and foremost, to "conserve the scenery" of the nation. On a clear day when the lake is still, there are few better places than this to experience beauty. Find a spot on the point, the bluff, or the lakeshore and let it sink in.

From the point, continue west along the sandy bluffs. The trail eventually turns right into the forest. Here, 300 year old lodgepole pine trees are surrounded by others that are dead and down and have fallen into decay, while new saplings grow in any patch of sunlight they can find.

At the forest's edge, the trail crosses another footbridge into an open sagebrush flat before returning to Indian Pond.

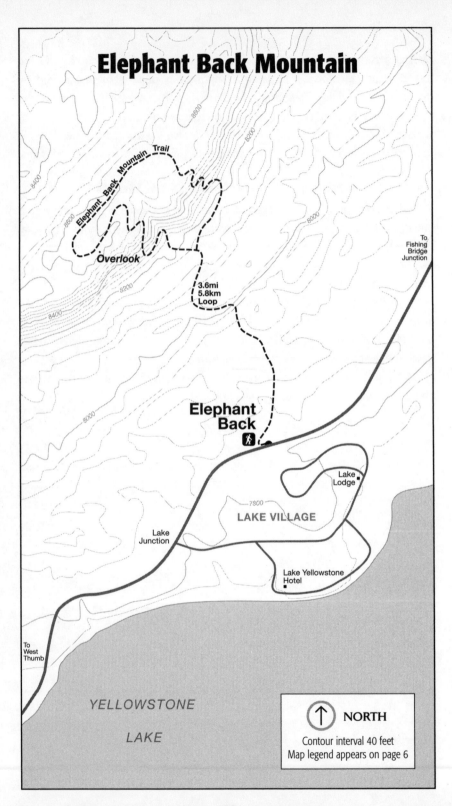

Elephant Back Mountain

Elephant Back Mountain Trail

8600

8200

8000

To
Fishing
Bridge
Junction

8400

8600

Overlook

8200

3.6mi
5.8km
Loop

8400

8000

**Elephant
Back**

Lake
Lodge

7800

LAKE VILLAGE

Lake
Junction

Lake Yellowstone
Hotel

To
West
Thumb

YELLOWSTONE

LAKE

↑ NORTH

Contour interval 40 feet
Map legend appears on page 6

...no other lake in North America of equal area
lies so high as the Yellowstone, or gives birth to so noble a river.
—Naturalist John Muir, 1885

19

Elephant Back Mountain

If you're looking for a grand view with a moderate output of energy and time, Elephant Back Mountain is an excellent choice. Traveling up an ancient lava flow, the trail climbs somewhat steeply for a short distance through a dense forest before reaching the summit, revealing an exquisite panoramic view of Yellowstone Lake. *See Plate 19.*

Level of difficulty: Moderate

Distance: 3.6-mile loop (5.8 km)

Elevation change: A total gain of 800 feet in 1.5 miles, with 600 feet in 0.8 miles

Duration: $1\frac{1}{2}$ - $2\frac{1}{2}$ hours

Best time of year: Late June through September. Though there is no official closure of this trail in spring, grizzly bears may be passing through the area on their way to the spawning streams around the lake. Inquire at the Fishing Bridge Visitor Center about recent bear sightings and possible closures of this trail. Also in spring, snow may still blanket the higher reaches of the 8,600-foot Elephant Back Mountain.

Trailhead: This hike begins at the pullout on the west side of the road, 1 mile (1.6 km) south of Fishing Bridge Junction and 0.5 mile (.8 km) north of Lake Junction.

Hiking directions: Follow the trail south, paralleling the road for about 50 yards, until it turns right leading into the forest. For the first mile of the hike, the trail is relatively flat, gaining only 200 feet before reaching the junction with the loop trail. The left fork of the loop is the shorter and less steep ascent. From the junction, the trail to the left climbs 600 feet in 0.8 mile on a series of switchbacks through the forest to the summit of Elephant Back Mountain. From the overlook, the trail continues in a loop, back down the mountain to the loop junction and out to the trailhead.

Naturalist notes: The trail up Elephant Back begins in an old-growth lodgepole pine forest. You'll note the 200 to 300 year old trees with few to no limbs on the lower part of their trunks. Lodgepole pines are self pruning trees. Growing close together, trees lose lower branches as they receive less sunlight. It's not hard to imagine why Plains Indian tribes used this tree in building their teepees, hence the name, lodgepole. You may be surprised that trees of this advanced age are so small in diameter. Things grow slowly in this volcanic soil!

You'll notice that the forest floor is strewn with dead and downed lodgepole pines. These trees have no taproot and become top-heavy in these shallow soils. Therefore, they're easily blown over by wind or toppled by gravity. Since Yellowstone has such a cold and dry climate, it takes a long time for dead trees to decompose. This is one of the forests in the park that didn't burn in 1988. The shade-tolerant spruces and firs, the climax forest here, will prevail, growing up under the dense forest canopy provided by aging lodgepoles. In the event of fire, the canopy is burned away and more sunlight reaches the forest floor, favoring sun-loving lodgepoles, and the cycle of forest succession begins again. On this gradual incline through the trees, look for porcupines that live in this wooded habitat. They may be watching you warily! The trail passes through a small wetland. Several logs along the trail will help you navigate this boggy area in the early season.

It's thought that fur trapper Jim Bridger originated the name "Elephant Back," although he was probably referring to Mount Washburn, which more obvious-ly resembles the humped back of an elephant than does the gentle slope of the mountain you're now climbing. On his famous geological survey through Yellowstone, Dr. Ferdinand Hayden took the name from the maps of an earlier expedition and applied it to this peak.

After a mile, you reach the junction with the loop trail. Take the left fork, which is less steep. Along the way, you'll notice flecks of shining black volcanic glass called obsidian that speak of the park's eruptive past. While resting on the long switchbacks, you'll have plenty of time to ponder the events that created this mountain and the magnificent lake you're about to see. This deep forest holds its secret well, as you'll catch only a few glimpses of this great lake through the openings in the trees on your way up.

At the top, the vast expanses of Yellowstone Lake unfold before you. The lake stretches out like the palm of a hand, with its four fingers (called "arms") and a large thumb, known as West Thumb. Only two of these arms are visible from Elephant Back. The other two and the Thumb are hidden by promonto-ries along the lakeshore.

Geologists believe that a massive volcano erupted and then collapsed here 640,000 years ago, leaving a huge hole in the ground, known as a "caldera." You don't see this large depression today because, over hundreds of thousands of years, successive lava flows largely filled it in. Elephant Back Mountain is one of the most recent of those lava flows, dating back 70,000 years. One part of the caldera that didn't completely fill with lava became Yellowstone Lake. The long narrow South and Southeast arms of the lake were carved out by the most recent glaciers, a huge sheet of ice, 4,000 feet thick, some 12,000 years ago. But now it's time to enjoy the present beauty of this grand lake, molded by lava and sculpted by ice. Rest on the log benches and take in this fine view.

In 1871, Dr. Hayden, who gave this mountain its name, was sent on expedition by Congress to confirm the wonders of the Yellowstone region reported by mountain men and previous exploring parties. His account of what he saw would eventually play a major role in the establishment of Yellowstone as the world's first national park. This was his impression of Yellowstone Lake: *The lake lay before us, a vast sheet of quiet water, of a most delicate marine hue, one of the most beautiful scenes I have ever beheld...Such a vision is worth a lifetime, and only one of such marvelous beauty will ever greet human eyes.* Perhaps you'll find that his words still hold true today.

Many prominent landmarks can be identified from this vantage point. To the far right are the sheltered waters near Bridge Bay with the Red Mountains looming beyond. Three of the lake's five islands are visible from here: the nearest is Stevenson; the largest is Frank; and smallest in view is Dot Island. Historic Lake Village lies directly in front of you, at the heart of which is the park's oldest remaining lodge, the famous yellow Lake Hotel. The peaks of the Absaroka Range tower in the distance, creating the eastern boundary of the park. Particularly prominent is the broad ridge of Avalanche Peak. On a cool morning, you may see the steam swirling up from Steamboat Point, which separates two large bays on the north shore of the lake. Here you will also see the effects of the East and Grizzly fires, which burned 24,000 acres when lightning struck the area in the summer of 2003. A large sandbar marks the point where Pelican Creek meets the lake. This creek flows through the large open Pelican Valley, home to the threatened grizzly bear. To the far left you see the Yellowstone River as it flows in a lazy meander on the beginning of its journey to meet the Missouri, and later the Mississippi, and then on to the Gulf of Mexico. It's the longest free flowing river left in the lower 48 states, a symbol of wildness preserved. Naturalist John Muir wrote of it:

...the river issues from the north side [of the lake] in a broad, smooth, stately current, silently gliding with such serene majesty that one fancies it knows the vast journey of four thousand miles that lies before it, and the work it has to do.

To return, follow the loop beyond the overlook down to the trail junction and retrace your steps back to the trailhead. A sign near the end of the trail directs park employees to their housing area and visitors toward the Lake Lodge cabins, which will bring you back to the trailhead.

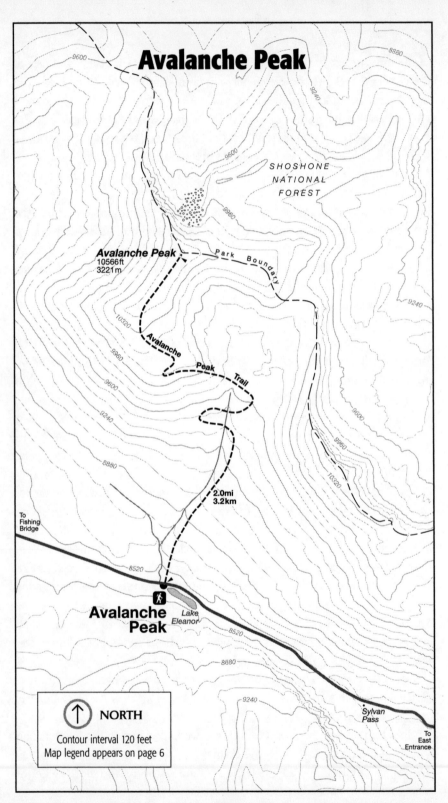

Avalanche Peak

*SHOSHONE
NATIONAL
FOREST*

Park   Boundary

Avalanche Peak
10566ft
3221m

Avalanche

Peak   Trail

2.0mi
3.2km

To
Fishing
Bridge

**Avalanche
Peak**

*Lake
Eleanor*

*Sylvan
Pass*

To
East
Entrance

NORTH

Contour interval 120 feet
Map legend appears on page 6

The air is electric and full of ozone, healing, reviving, exhilarating, kept pure by frost and fire, while the scenery is wild enough to awaken the dead.

—Naturalist John Muir, 1885

20

Avalanche Peak

For a truly breathtaking encounter with the wild side of Yellowstone, make the steep and rugged ascent above timberline to the knife-edged summit of Avalanche Peak. Here, in the heart of the Absaroka Range, you'll be afforded stunning views of some of the park's tallest and most remote peaks and the glistening blue waters of Yellowstone Lake. *See Plate 20.*

Level of Difficulty: Strenuous

Distance: 4 miles round trip (6.4 km)

Elevation change: A gain of 2,100 feet in 2 miles

Duration: 3 - 4 hours

Best time of year: Mid-July through August. Since snow can cover the trail well into summer, it's best to hike Avalanche Peak after mid-July when the snow has receded and the wildflowers are blooming. In fall, grizzly bears frequent this area, seeking out the whitebark pine for its nutritious seeds.

Trailhead: This hike begins in the parking area at the west end of Lake Eleanor on the south side of the road, 19 miles (30.4 km) east of Fishing Bridge Junction and 8 miles (12.8 km) west of the East Entrance.

Hiking directions: From the parking area at Lake Eleanor, carefully cross the road and enter the forest where the trail begins its steep ascent up the mountain. In just over a mile, you'll arrive at the base of the large amphitheater bowl of Avalanche Peak. Continue to the left, climbing over talus slopes on the mountain's southern flank. After switchbacking to the right, the trail reaches an open level area below the summit. You'll see a number of trails in the talus climbing the short distance to the ridge. The safest path is the one farthest to your left. To return to the trailhead, retrace your route.

Special attention: The trail to Avalanche Peak is exceptionally rocky and steep. It leads to a narrow, exposed ridge above timberline. Sturdy hiking boots are recommended, particularly on the talus slopes. The summit can be cold and windy, even on days that are warm at lower elevations. Be prepared for quickly changing weather conditions by bringing along adequate warm clothing, and wind- and raingear. Hiking in the morning is advisable, before afternoon storms build and the danger of lightning increases.

Naturalist notes: At 10,566 feet, Avalanche Peak cuts an impressive figure along the eastern boundary of the park. From a distance, the peak is distinguished from its more jagged neighbors by the broad, flat, knife-edge ridge that defines its summit.

The trail enters the forest and immediately begins its rugged ascent up the mountain, ambitiously climbing 2,100 feet in 2 miles to the summit. Avalanche Peak is part of the Absaroka Range, home to the park's tallest mountains and most remote wilderness. Originally referred to by early explorers as the Yellowstone or Snowy Range, these mountains were rechristened by geologist Arnold Hague in 1885 in recognition of the neighboring Crow Indians. The word "Absaroka" is the name these Native Americans use to refer to themselves. It has been translated to mean people of the "large beaked bird," "forked-tail bird," "bird people," or "sparrowhawk people." At some point in history, the name "Crow" emerged and its usage has survived into the present day.

As the trail climbs, it travels through a wonderfully lush forest of Engelmann spruce and subalpine fir, paralleling a small creek to your left. The sound of the flowing water and the lovely setting help to take your mind off the serious elevation you're gaining. After climbing for about 0.75 mile, the trail levels off and drops into a small meadow, crossing the streambed you've been following. From this meadow, you can see the north face of Top Notch Peak to the south. In late July and early August, this meadow explodes in a profusion of colorful wildflowers. Along the trail, look for the yellow columbine, the tall purple larkspur, bluebells, Indian paintbrush, mountain gentian, geranium, and heartleaf arnica, among others.

Across the meadow, the trail bends to the left and climbs again, returning into the forest. Paralleling the mountain for a short distance is a swath cut through the forest with trees in various stages of regrowth, attesting to the periodic avalanches that strike this precipitous terrain and give the mountain its name. Imagine a heavy load of snow powering its way down the slope, flattening the forest and leaving this scar in its wake. Notice the young trees struggling to get established here. Looking upslope and across to Top Notch Peak, you will also see patches of orange trees affected by blisterust

The trail soon enters the whitebark pine forest, through which it begins to switchback. This spacious pine forest is a rare treat, not found on most Yellowstone day hikes. The whitebark pine is a high altitude tree, favoring elevations above 8,000 feet to timberline, near 10,000 feet. This five-needled pine is distinguished by its whitish bark. It produces a distinctive purple cone whose seed or "nut" is a favorite and very nutritious source of food for the grizzly bear in the fall. Because of the bears' affinity for the whitebark pine nut, Avalanche Peak is a good trail to avoid late in the season. The loss of many of these trees to blisterust presents a concern to the long-term survival of grizzlies in Yellowstone.

After traveling a little over a mile, the trail emerges from the forest to a most impressive spot, the amphitheater bowl of Avalanche Peak. While catching your breath, this is a good place to admire the scouring effects of the glacier that sculpted this dramatic peak.

From here, the trail crosses through talus slopes all the way to the summit. Talus is an assortment of loose angular rock usually found at the base of a steep slope or cliff. Little by little, the mountain is being broken apart by the weathering action of frost—the freezing and thawing of water within the cracks of the rock. Be careful as you maneuver among these talus slopes; the rocks can be quite loose and unstable. The trail ascends the peak's southern flank and switchbacks sharply to the right, climbing to a second open area before the final short ascent to the top. You'll notice several trails in the talus slope leading to the summit. The most gradual and safe route is farthest to your left as you face the mountain.

This precarious perch affords views of some of the most stirring high country scenery you'll find in the park. To the southeast, Yellowstone Lake lies before you like a sapphire set in mountains—and what mountains they are! Tall, rugged peaks surround you. The Absarokas are a masterpiece of nature's handiwork, born of the fires within the earth, then sculpted by glaciers. About 50 million years ago, these peaks were erupting volcanoes during an active period of mountain building in the Rocky Mountains. Ashflows and volcanic debris rained down, preserving Yellowstone's fossil forests and creating this high chain of mountains that form the park's eastern boundary.

Ice played a crucial role in molding the appearance of the mountains we see today. From the top of Avalanche, you can learn classic lessons in glaciation. The peak's large bowls, directly below you to the southwest and east, are cirques, where glaciers were born. As ice accumulated, it began to flow down under its own weight, scouring and sculpting amphitheater-shaped depressions on both sides of the mountain. The ridge between them is called an "arete." Look for other signs of the last ice age in the form of cirques and U-shaped valleys associated with glaciers. The power of ice is evident everywhere you look. You will also see the effects of fire. In the summer of 2003, lightning struck just west of Avalanche Peak, starting a fire that burned thousands of acres and threatened the villages of Fishing Bridge and the East Entrance.

Snowcapped most of the summer, Avalanche Peak and the Absaroka Range provide some of the most magnificent mountain scenery in the park. A formidable geographic barrier along the park's eastern boundary, the southern reaches of the range in Yellowstone comprise the largest, most remote area of wilderness remaining in the lower 48 states. During his 1885 visit, naturalist John Muir captured the essence of such a place when he wrote:

The air is electric and full of ozone, healing, reviving, exhilarating, kept pure by frost and fire, while the scenery is wild enough to awaken the dead. It is a glorious place to grow in and rest in;...up in the fountain hollows of the ancient glaciers between the peaks, where cool pools and brooks and gardens of precious plants charmingly embowered are never wanting, and good rough rocks with every variety of cliff and scaur are invitingly near for outlooks and exercise.

Take a moment to contemplate the wild nature of this vast landscape around you. After enjoying these dramatic views, retrace your steps down the mountain to the trailhead at Eleanor Lake.

21

*Nestled among the forest-crowned hills...lay this inland sea,
its crystal waves dancing and sparkling in the sunlight, as if
laughing with joy for their wild freedom.*
—Explorer David Folsom, 1869

Lake Overlook

True to its name, this short hike affords an outstanding overlook of the West Thumb of Yellowstone Lake. This pleasant foray through forest and meadow will reveal the dramatic saga of the fire that burned here in 1988 and also of the fire within the earth that molded and formed this volcanic landscape. *See Plate 21.*

Level of difficulty: Easy

Distance: 2-mile loop (3.2 km)

Elevation change: A gain of 200 feet in 0.25 mile

Duration: 1 - 2 hours

Best time of year: Late June through September. In spring, grizzly bears may pass through this area as they travel between the spawning creeks around the West Thumb of Yellowstone Lake. Inquire at the Grant Village Visitor Center about recent bear sightings in the area before hiking this trail then.

Trailhead: This hike starts at the beginning of the West Thumb Geyser Basin parking area.

Hiking directions: Follow the orange trail markers away from the parking area toward the South Entrance Road. In several hundred yards, you'll cross this road and head into the forest. Soon, you'll meet the junction with the loop trail. Take the right fork across a small creek on a log bridge. Upon reaching some dormant thermal features, the trail turns sharply left. Then, it climbs steeply up a hill, paralleling several more thermal features as it ascends to the overlook. From this point, the trail continues down through a long narrow meadow and bends to the left, back into the forest. It meanders through the trees and then crosses a small wetland, where it rejoins the junction with the loop trail. Continue straight and cross the road to return to the West Thumb Geyser Basin.

Naturalist notes: The Lake Overlook Trail is a nice one to take in conjunction with a walk around the West Thumb Geyser Basin. From the trailhead, this hike crosses the road near West Thumb Junction. Had you been standing at this point on July 31, 1988, you would have witnessed a wall of fire rising up over

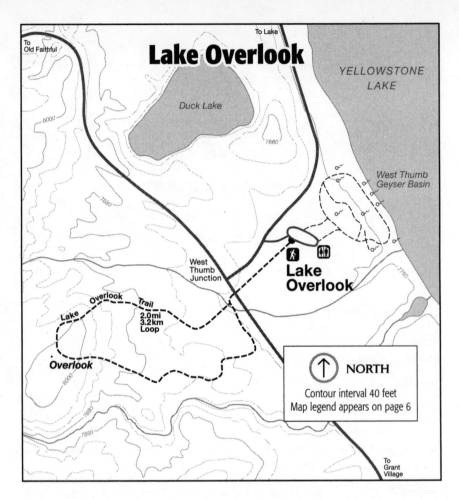

Lake Overlook

To Lake

To
Old Faithful

YELLOWSTONE
LAKE

Duck Lake

8000

7880

West Thumb
Geyser Basin

West
Thumb
Junction

Lake
Overlook

Overlook Trail

Lake

2.0mi
3.2km
Loop

Overlook

8000

7880

7880

NORTH

Contour interval 40 feet
Map legend appears on page 6

To
Grant
Village

the crest of the ridge ahead of you. Driven by high winds, the flames leapt over the road, burning down to the shores of Yellowstone Lake. It was a memorable day in a now famous fire season.

As the trail leads into the forest, you'll see the role fire plays in forest succession. Notice the many young lodgepole pines sprouting up where Engelmann spruce and subalpine fir once grew. By burning away the shaded forest canopy these trees provided, the fires allowed more sunlight to reach the forest floor. The sun loving lodgepole is replacing the shade tolerant spruce and fir as the next generation of forest here.

While news of the major fires burning in Yellowstone was shocking people all over the world, scientists had long known that cataclysmic fires such as this burn through the largely lodgepole forest of the Yellowstone Plateau every 200 to 400 years. In fact, lodgepole forests are intended to burn. Some of their cones are "serotinous," which means they need the intense heat of fire to open and release their seeds.

You'll notice that the flames skipped across the land, burning some stands of trees and not others. This creates what biologists call a "mosaic" or patchwork pattern of burned and unburned forests. The diversity of habitat that results becomes home to a larger variety of birds and animals than existed in pre-fire days. In the burned areas, new grasses flourish, creating excellent browse for animals such as deer and elk. You may see them along the trail, especially if you're hiking around dawn or dusk. Despite the biological benefits of fire, it's hard to dispute the fact that a burned forest is a bit unsightly. While it may not be pretty, it is natural, and that's what the national parks are trying to preserve.

The trail eventually turns left and follows a line of remnant thermal features up the hill to the summit. These mostly dormant hot springs and mudpots hint at the great heat source that lies beneath the ground. At the overlook, rest on the wooden bench and enjoy the terrific view of West Thumb. While the fires of 1988 seared the surface of the land here, it's the fires that seethe within the earth that forged the face of this volcanic plateau and created the nearly circular body of water that lies before you.

West Thumb derives its name from the fact that Yellowstone Lake is shaped roughly like an outstretched hand, of which this large bay is the thumb. It's equal in size to Crater Lake, in another national park, and was formed in a similarly explosive way.

Yellowstone lies on a restless part of earth's crust. Some geologists believe that a plume of heat rises up from a "hotspot" in the mantle of the earth below, causing the lower part of the earth's crust to melt into molten rock, known as magma. This magma may be as near as 1 to 5 miles beneath your feet. As the magma rises, the ground above it is forced upward, causing it to bulge, much like a blister forming on the earth's surface. Eventually, the land is stretched so thin that it cracks. These cracks descend deeper and deeper, until they penetrate the magma chamber.

This resulted in one of the largest eruptions in the history of the world. Volcanic ash covered thousands of square miles in a matter of minutes and was carried across much of the continent. Smoke covered the sun for so long that it cooled the world's climate. This was truly a world changing event.

As the ash blew out from the sides, there was nothing to support the roof of the magma chamber, so it collapsed, leaving a massive depression in the earth, known as a caldera. This, the third in a succession of major volcanic eruptions in this area, occurred 640,000 years ago, creating a caldera 47 miles long, 28 miles wide, and several thousand feet deep. As a visitor to Yellowstone today, you may wonder why you don't see this huge hole in the ground. Lava flows continued to ooze from the earth, filling this deep depression to create the volcanic plateau that comprises much of Yellowstone. A smaller eruption occurred 150,000 years ago. The caldera it created filled with water, rather than lava. This caldera is the West Thumb of Yellowstone Lake, which you see before you.

After pondering this explosive encounter, take a quiet moment to enjoy the grand view. In the distance, the impressive peaks of the Absaroka Range rise above the eastern shore of the lake. Mount Sheridan looms high to your right, standing at the southern edge of the 640,000 year old caldera. To your left, the summits of Observation Peak and Mount Washburn barely peek over the wooded ridges of the volcanic plateau. These mountains mark the northern boundary of the Yellowstone caldera.

Explorer David Folsom, on expedition here in 1869, had this to say of the view from a point near here:

As we were...departing on our homeward trip, we ascended the summit of a neighboring hill, and took one final look at Yellowstone Lake. Nestled among the forest-crowned hills...lay this inland sea, its crystal waves dancing and sparkling in the sunlight, as if laughing with joy for their wild freedom.

Wild freedom. Perhaps this captures best the purpose of the national parks —to preserve wildlife, wildlands, wild processes, and freedom to enjoy them.

After taking in the views from the overlook, follow the trail down through the long meadow until it bends left into the forest. Meander through both the old forest untouched by fire and the dense growth of young lodgepole pines born of fire. As the road comes into view, the trail turns left and passes through a small wetland before it reaches the junction with the loop trail. Continue straight, cross the road, and return to the trailhead.

If you haven't already taken the short walk around the West Thumb Geyser Basin, do so. Its setting on the shoreline affords more magnificent views of Yellowstone Lake and the Absarokas beyond. Some of the park's deepest and most beautiful hot springs, Abyss and Black Pool, are found here as well as the famous Fishing Cone. An historic ranger station, built in 1925, sits at the top of the geyser basin. Reminiscent of an earlier era, it serves today as a Yellowstone Association bookstore in summer and a warming hut in winter.

22

"Lake Riddle" is a fugitive name, which has been located at several places, but nowhere permanently. It is supposed to have been used originally to designate the mythical lake, among the mountains…whence… water flowed to both oceans.—Explorer Frank Bradley, 1872

Riddle Lake

Take this delightful walk in the woods amid small streams and flowering wet meadows to the tranquil waters of this little mountain lake—a place where moose may lurk and birds abound. With Mount Sheridan watching over you, search for the answer to the "riddle" of Riddle Lake. *See Plate 22.*

Level of difficulty: Moderate

Distance: 5 miles round trip (8 km)

Elevation change: Minimal

Duration: 2 - 3 hours

Best time of year: Mid-July through September. As part of a bear management area, the Riddle Lake Trail is closed during the first part of the summer. It opens each year on July 15. Be alert for bears at any time of season.

Trailhead: This hike begins from the pullout on the east side of the road just past the Continental Divide sign, 2.5 miles (4 km) south of the Grant Village intersection on the South Entrance Road.

Hiking directions: From the trailhead, follow the trail 2.5 miles to the north shore of Riddle Lake. Return to the trailhead by the same route.

Naturalist notes: The Riddle Lake Trail is one of the most intimate hiking experiences in Yellowstone. Everything about it feels personal, from the nurturing forests that shelter tiny flower-filled meadows, to the lake itself, which lies peacefully in the protective shadow of Mount Sheridan.

Because this hike begins so close to the Continental Divide, one might assume that it could be strenuous, with lots of ups and downs. To the contrary, it's probably one of the most level trails in the park. Shortly after leaving the trailhead, you'll cross over the divide, although you probably won't notice it. Running atop the ridgelines of the rolling terrain of southern Yellowstone, the divide passes through with little fanfare, unless, of course, you're a drop of water. Then, the consequences are profound.

The Continental Divide is the ridgeline atop the mountains of the West that determines where streams, rivers and lakes ultimately flow. If rain or snow falls

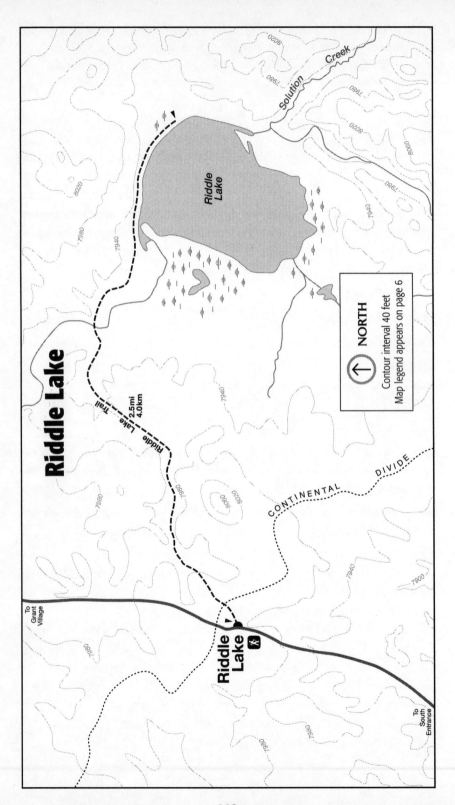

Riddle Lake

Riddle
Lake

Solution Creek

Riddle Lake Trail
2.5mi
4.0km

CONTINENTAL DIVIDE

NORTH

Contour interval 40 feet
Map legend appears on page 6

To Grant Village

Riddle Lake

To South Entrance

on the east side of the divide, it will eventually find its way via the Missouri and Mississippi rivers to the Atlantic Ocean. If it falls on the west side, it will end up in the Pacific Ocean by way of the Snake and Columbia rivers. Yellowstone could be considered the headwaters of the nation. As naturalist John Muir observed, here in this *big, wholesome wilderness on the broad summit of the Rocky Mountains…the greatest of the American rivers take their rise.* The Snake, the Yellowstone, and the headwaters of the Missouri, among others, owe their origins to the snows that fall on this high plateau. Riddle Lake does its part, too, contributing to the Yellowstone River system by feeding into Yellowstone Lake. Its location near the great divide is the cause of a riddle that confounded early explorers for years. This "riddle" will be revealed at the end of the Naturalist Notes.

The hike begins by entering a forest that has been touched by flames. The effects of the fires are not widespread, however. The burned areas blend in with the unburned areas. Live trees mingle with dead ones, creating a patchwork, or "mosaic," pattern of burn. This is common when a fire skips on the wind across the land. As you hike the trail, you'll see evidence of such fire behavior.

The forests here are mostly lodgepole pine in varying degrees of succession. Younger and older forests abound. Now and then, where fire has had greater effect, a whole new generation of young lodgepoles has sprouted up. First, you'll see trees comprising a classic old-growth lodgepole pine forest. These lodgepoles are tall with no lower branches, almost like telephone poles. Little by little, these old trees give way to the more shade-loving spruce and fir. Notice the occasional large spruce surrounded by variously aged younger trees. If you look closely, you may also see a few young whitebark pine, which can be distinguished from the lodgepole by its clusters of five needles and its smooth light bark.

Farther along the trail, the forest changes to a stand of younger lodgepoles, 40 to 50 feet tall. Lacking sunlight, their lower branches are beginning to die back, part of the self-pruning process they undergo as they mature. Notice the black hair-like lichen hanging among the branches. Commonly known as "old man's beard," this lichen does no harm to the tree; it simply finds these dying branches a great place to obtain sunlight and moisture.

In the dappled light these young and old forests provide, the ground is covered with grasses, dwarf huckleberry, and flowers such as the purple lupine and the yellow heartleaf arnica. The beauty of this trail is its diversity. It meanders through forests and also crosses intermittent streams and small meadows. In the moist soils of the meadows, wildflowers abound with names like shooting star, monkshood, and elephanthead. If you get down and take a close look at these flowers, you'll quickly understand where their names originate. The shooting star hangs seemingly suspended in air, while the monkshood blossom is shrouded in a hood-like flower. As for the elephant head, it's clear whose face is shining back at you.

The only elephant you'll find here is in the head of a flower, but these meadows are the haunts of another charismatic creature, the moose. The largest members of the deer family, moose favor marshy areas like these meadows and the shallow waters of streams, ponds, or lakeshores such as Riddle Lake. In the summer, they feed largely on willows growing around water. However, should the aquatic plants growing beneath the surface look particularly appetizing, moose have the ability to submerge completely, swimming underwater, even with a full rack of antlers, which can weigh up to 80 pounds.

With its long, gangly legs and large, almost horse-like face, the moose is one of nature's most unusual looking creations. Some rangers quip that this was the only animal designed by a committee. A mature bull moose can easily top 1,000 pounds and tower well over 6 feet tall, making it second only to the bison as the park's largest animal. They are distinguished by a dewlap or "bell" hanging from their neck and the broad, palmate antlers on the males. As you cross the meadows, look for these often solitary creatures.

In about 2 miles, the forests and meadows open at the shore of Riddle Lake and the large marsh that lies adjacent to its western edge. This 274-acre lake is home to the native cutthroat trout. You may also find more moose grazing along the marshy shoreline. This is wonderful habitat for water birds, too. Plying the watery wilderness of the lake may be the American white pelican, bald eagle, osprey, common loon, and sandhill crane.

Riddle Lake has a puzzling history. The name originated from stories of fur trappers that somewhere in these mountains was a lake situated astride the Continental Divide, whose waters fed both oceans. In 1872, this "mythical lake among the mountains," inspired Frank Bradley of the second Hayden Geological Survey to solve the "riddle" of this "two-ocean water" by attaching the name Riddle to this small lake which he believed sat upon the divide. In truth, Riddle Lake lies very near the Divide, within a mile in fact, but not directly upon it. As to where its waters actually drain, look no farther than its eastern shore. The appropriately named Solution Creek solves the riddle as it delivers the lake's waters to Yellowstone Lake, placing Riddle Lake on the eastern side of the divide.

Oddly enough, the name "riddle" probably never originally referred to the question of where the lake's waters flowed. It stems, rather, from a simple mapping error. It seems the Lewis and Clark map of 1806 identified Jackson Lake in the Grand Tetons as Lake Biddle. Later, another cartographer misinterpreted this as Lake Riddle. To add to the confusion, subsequent maps moved the name to Yellowstone. Bradley thought this "fugitive name" deserved a permanent home. In this lake, he thought he'd found an appropriate reply to the early fur trappers' stories.

Several "two-ocean" waters do exist in the park, but not at Riddle Lake. One is on the Two Ocean Plateau in the southeastern part of the park. The other is Isa Lake, which you'll see as you drive over Craig Pass between West Thumb and Old Faithful.

The trail continues for about another 0.5 mile along the northern shoreline of the lake. With lily pads floating on its surface and the Red Mountains framed in the distance to the south, Riddle Lake is an ideal setting to sit, rest, and contemplate the many "riddles" that life presents each one of us. These cloistered forests, secluded meadows, and the sanctuary of the lake can offer the kind of retreat found only in nature. Ralph Waldo Emerson knew of the healing power of the natural world when he wrote: *In the woods we return to reason and faith. There I feel that nothing can befall me in life,—no disgrace, no calamity…which nature cannot repair.* If you look closely, you may just find the answers to the riddles of your life reflected in these tranquil waters.

To return, retrace your steps back to the trailhead.

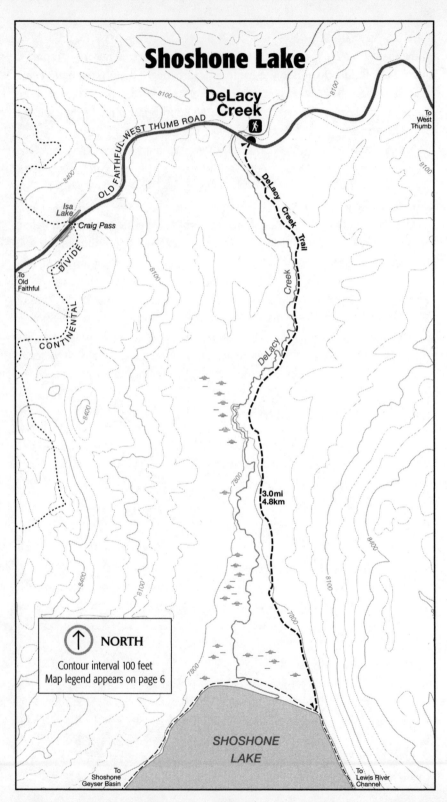

Shoshone Lake

DeLacy
Creek

To
West
Thumb

OLD FAITHFUL-WEST THUMB ROAD

DeLacy Creek Trail

8100

8100

8100

8400

Isa
Lake

Craig Pass

DIVIDE

To
Old
Faithful

CONTINENTAL

8400

8100

DeLacy Creek

7800

3.0mi
4.8km

8400

8100

7800

NORTH

Contour interval 100 feet
Map legend appears on page 6

7800

8100

7800

SHOSHONE
LAKE

To
Shoshone
Geyser Basin

To
Lewis River
Channel

[It]…is a very fine view of mountain scenery. Steeply down several miles of pine clad mountain slopes lay Shoshone Lake, a deep blue gem in a somber setting of pines.

—Park visitors Alfred and Estella Bell, 1904

PARK TRAIL

Shoshone Lake

Shoshone Lake is Yellowstone's most popular backcountry destination. Get a taste for the wilderness on this delightful hike through forest and meadow. Follow DeLacy Creek to this large mountain lake tucked in the pines. *See Plate 23.*

Level of difficulty: Moderate

Distance: 6 miles round trip (9.6 km)

Elevation change: Minimal

Duration: 2 - 3 hours

Best time of year: Mid-June through September.

Trailhead: This hike begins at the parking area for the DeLacy Creek Trailhead on the north side of the road, 8.6 miles (13.8 km) west of West Thumb Junction and 8.9 miles (14.3 km) east of the Old Faithful overpass on the Old Faithful-West Thumb Road. Do not confuse this with the nearby DeLacy Creek Picnic Area.

Hiking directions: From the parking area, carefully cross the road and begin at the DeLacy Creek Trailhead sign. Follow the trail along the creek for 3 miles to the north shore of Shoshone Lake. Return to the trailhead by the same route.

Naturalist notes: This gentle hike through meadow and forest has a grand destination, the park's largest backcountry lake. This "deep blue gem" is remote, accessible only by foot or by canoe. In fact, the U.S. Fish and Wildlife Service has deemed Shoshone Lake the largest lake in the lower 48 that cannot be reached by road. The DeLacy Creek Trail is the most direct route to this big lake in the wilds.

The hike begins by winding pleasantly downhill through a lodgepole pine forest. This forest, typical of those in Yellowstone, opens a window into the past. It represents what many of the park's forests looked like prior to the dramatic changes brought about by the 1988 fires. Soon, DeLacy Creek appears on the right. Its lazy meanders will accompany you on your journey to the lake.

The lodgepole pine, aptly named for its historical use among Native Americans in building teepees, is the dominant tree here. Growing in open sunny areas, lodgepoles mature into a dense forest. As they grow taller, their lower branches are shaded and naturally prune away, leaving a 200 to 300 year old forest of tall and slender trees. In these older forests, little sunlight reaches the forest floor, resulting in a relatively sparse understory and little browse for wildlife. On this trail, however, you'll find one ground cover that manages well in the shade of the lodgepole, the low lying grouse whortleberry, or dwarf huckleberry. In these dense forests, the more shade-loving spruce and fir can get established. They will eventually become the dominant, or climax, species. However, with natural processes always at work, things never remain constant. When a fire burns through these forests, the open, sunny sites it creates favor the rebirth of the lodgepole over the spruce and fir. Though fire didn't reach this part of Yellowstone in 1988, this lodgepole forest was born of similar fires several centuries earlier.

After about a mile, the trail emerges from the forest into the meadows along DeLacy Creek. For the remaining 2 miles to the lake, the trail skirts along the edge of the forest, passing through meadows and crossing a few small streams feeding DeLacy Creek. Enjoy the many flowers blooming at the forest's edge. As you get closer to Shoshone Lake, the view opens up, offering a glimpse of the lake in the distance. The expansive feeling these meadows evoke nicely complements the occasional forays back into the forest. As you gaze across the meadows, watch for wildlife. Elk, mule deer, and especially moose often graze here, usually in the cooler hours of morning and early evening. Coyotes, too, are sometimes seen hunting here.

Another prominent resident of these wet meadows is the elegant sandhill crane. With its long legs and long neck, it can reach the height of a deer, standing up to 4 feet tall. The melodic lilt of its call and the distinctive red patch on its head distinguish it from its rarer and larger cousin, the endangered whooping crane, and the more common great blue heron.

Shortly before it reaches the lake, the trail returns to the forest. Soon, DeLacy Creek reappears on the right as does Shoshone Lake ahead. The creek delivers its waters as a wide, meandering stream lined with lily pads. The forest opens and the full expanse of this large mountain lake is revealed.

Shoshone Lake lies in a basin surrounded mostly by forest. Large and cold, it covers 8,050 acres with a maximum depth of 205 feet. Its colors range from a lovely aquamarine in the shallow areas near shore to a rich dark blue where it suddenly deepens. Reflected in these waters, you'll see a lake of many moods. In the morning, it can be tranquil and still, but by afternoon, white caps may build and waves break onshore. The lake was naturally barren of fish due to the waterfalls downstream on the Lewis River. However, today, healthy populations of lake, brown, and brook trout are found here, a result of stocking efforts in the 1890s.

Throughout its history, Shoshone Lake has gone by a number of different names. Early fur trappers called it "Snake Lake," a nod to the neighboring Shoshone Indians who, at the time, were referred to as the Snake Indians. Later, in the 1860s, it was called "Madison Lake" because it was believed, incorrectly, to be the headwaters of the Madison River. Finally, members of the second Hayden Geological Survey in 1872 harkened back to the early Indian reference used by the mountain men. Frank Bradley of the Survey wrote: *Upon crossing the divide to the larger lake, we found it to belong to the Snake River drainage, and therefore called it Shoshone Lake, adopting the Indian name of the Snake [River].*

Many of Yellowstone's lakes, rivers, and streams lie on the eastern side of the Continental Divide, draining to the Gulf of Mexico and the Atlantic Ocean. Shoshone Lake is a notable exception. The Hayden Survey realized that the lake is situated on the western slope of the Continental Divide. It's the source of the Lewis River, which flows on to the Snake River, then to the Columbia and, finally, to the Pacific Ocean.

Where the trail meets the lake, there is a gravelly beach strewn with driftwood, the perfect place to relax with a picnic lunch and contemplate the beauty around you. You'll notice trails heading in both directions along the lakeshore, leading farther into the backcountry. To the right, the trail heads west, running the length of the lake to Shoshone Geyser Basin, 8.5 miles away. Heading left, the trail leads to the lake's outlet, the Lewis River Channel, and the Dogshead Trail in 4.2 miles. At this threshold of the wilderness, the words of Wallace Stegner come to mind:

We simply need...wild country available to us, even if we never do more than drive to its edge and look in. For it can be a means of reassuring ourselves of our sanity as creatures, a part of the geography of hope.

Shoshone Lake is a watery wilderness that reminds us of the beauty, the power, and ultimately the mystery of the natural world. This mystery, known by the native people for whom the lake is named, is revealed to us today in big wild places like Yellowstone.

When you're ready to leave its shore, follow DeLacy Creek back to the trailhead.

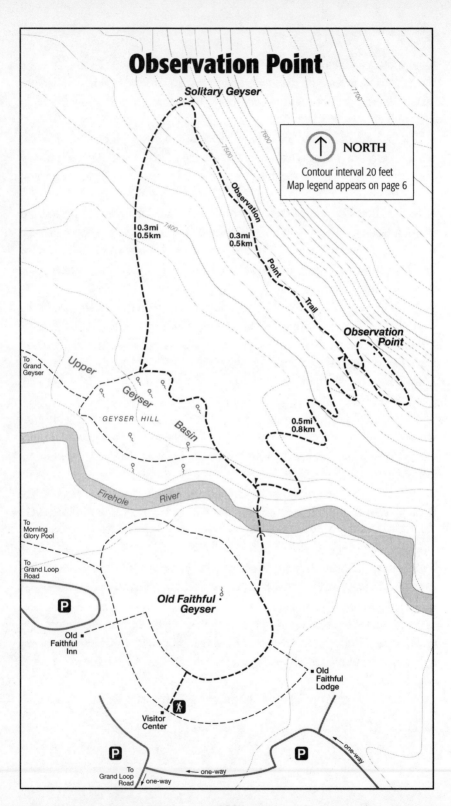

Observation Point

Solitary Geyser

Observation Point Trail

Observation Point

NORTH

Contour interval 20 feet
Map legend appears on page 6

7700

7600

7800

7400

0.3mi
0.5km

0.3mi
0.5km

0.5mi
0.8km

To
Grand
Geyser

Upper

Geyser

GEYSER HILL

Basin

Firehole River

To
Morning
Glory Pool

To
Grand Loop
Road

P

Old
Faithful
Inn

*Old Faithful
Geyser*

Old
Faithful
Lodge

Visitor
Center

P

To
Grand Loop
Road

one-way

one-way

P

one-way

...at no great distance before us, [we saw] an immense body of sparkling water, projected suddenly and with terrific force into the air... We had found a real geyser.

—Explorer Nathaniel Langford, 1870

(24)

Observation Point

Geologically speaking, the Upper Geyser Basin is one of the most extraordinary places on the planet. Over 25 percent of the world's geysers can be found here. Take this short steep walk to get an overview of this remarkable area. Enjoy an eruption of Old Faithful from this interesting vantage point. *See Plate 24.*

Level of difficulty: Moderate

Distance: 1.8-mile loop (2.9 km)

Elevation change: A gain of 160 feet in 0.5 mile

Duration: 1 - 2 hours

Best time of year: June through September.

Trailhead: This hike begins at the Old Faithful Visitor Center.

Hiking directions: From the visitor center, walk toward Old Faithful Geyser. Turn right on the boardwalk trail and follow it around the geyser. On the other side of Old Faithful, turn right to cross the Firehole River on a large footbridge. Soon, you'll reach the well marked junction with the Observation Point Trail. Turn right here and continue up the switchbacks to another junction in the trail. This is the loop trail to the overlook. Turn right on this trail and proceed to the overlook. Beyond the overlook, continue northwest, winding back down to the junction with the loop trail. From here, turn right and walk 0.3 mile to Solitary Geyser. From Solitary Geyser, follow the trail that goes down to Geyser Hill. Take the boardwalk trail to the left until it meets the paved trail leading back across the Firehole River to Old Faithful Geyser and the visitor center.

Special attention: If you'd like to see an eruption of Old Faithful from Observation Point, inquire at the Old Faithful Visitor Center for the next prediction time. Allow 30 minutes to get to Observation Point.

Naturalist notes: Follow the boardwalk to the right around Old Faithful and take the trail across the Firehole River. Pause on the bridge for a moment to enjoy this lovely stream, a quiet respite from the rush of humanity gathered to watch the famous geyser. Across the bridge, take the trail to the right toward

Observation Point. The trail winds through forest and marsh, crossing several footbridges and climbing steeply uphill before it meets the junction with the loop trail to the point.

As you gain elevation and begin to see the sweeping views, consider the dramatic events that occurred here on September 7, 1988. In perhaps the most searing firestorm of this now famous season, a 300-foot wall of fire blew over the ridge from the south, behind the visitor center. The sky was orange with fire and black with smoke. High winds blew burning embers in advance of the fire. Crews of firefighters stood poised to defend the area, especially the historic Old Faithful Inn. Minutes before the flames were about to engulf the inn, the wind made a sudden shift to the northeast, blazing, instead, up the hillside on which you now stand. When all was said and done, $120 million was spent battling the many fires that burned in and around Yellowstone that summer. It was the largest firefighting effort in the history of the nation. This succeeded in protecting human life and property, but made little impact on extinguishing the fires themselves. On September 11, a quarter inch of snow fell in Yellowstone. This, alone, contained the seven major fire complexes that raged across the landscape. Many lessons were learned from this experience. The national parks do not just preserve things, they preserve processes, even if those processes are beyond our control. Yellowstone is one of the last vestiges of wild America, where all the grand forces of nature are still at play. Maybe here, we learn a new humility, when we acknowledge that there are places that we not only could not, but should not control.

Soon, you'll meet the junction with the short loop trail that encircles Observation Point. Turn right and make the last sweeping turn up to the summit. While waiting for Old Faithful to erupt, imagine what it might've been like to be a member of the Washburn Expedition in 1870, stumbling unknowingly upon this geyser basin. After two weeks of arduous travel around the northern and eastern parts of what is today Yellowstone National Park, this intrepid group headed north over the present day Craig Pass on their journey home. On their way down the pass, they saw a plume of steam rising from the valley below. Of this day, Nathaniel Langford, who would later become a powerful proponent of the national park idea, wrote in his journal:

We had within a distance of fifty miles seen what we believed to be the greatest wonders on the continent…Judge, then, of our astonishment on entering this basin, to see at no great distance before us, an immense body of sparkling water, projected suddenly and with terrific force into the air… We had found a real geyser. In the valley before us were a thousand hot springs of various sizes and character… We gave such names to those…which we saw in action as we think will best illustrate the peculiarities. The one I have just described, General Washburn has named "Old Faithful" because of the regularity of its eruption.

The Washburn Expedition spent several days exploring this area and naming the features here. There were many to name. This is the largest concentration of geysers anywhere. Sixty percent of the world's geysers are in Yellowstone, 25 percent or 150 of them are in this one incredible square mile alone. There is no place on earth quite like this. From here, you may see eruptions of several of the geysers below: Lion, Beehive, Plume, and Castle. The star performer, of course, is Old Faithful. Hopefully, you'll find its showering play as enthralling as those who first discovered it. Old Faithful is neither the largest geyser, nor the most predictable, but it is spectacular, and it is still faithful.

Many people remember when the great geyser's interval was roughly 60 minutes. This was prior to the large earthquake at Hebgen Lake outside the park's west entrance in 1959. Old Faithful got the reputation of erupting "every hour on the hour," when, in fact, its interval had always varied, anywhere between 33 and 120 minutes throughout recorded history. Though earthquakes have changed the geyser's interval from time to time, it still remains predictable plus or minus 10 minutes. Old Faithful is predictable, in part, because geologists believe it doesn't share its underground water reservoir with any other geysers. Rangers predict the next eruption based on how long the previous one lasted. In a high-tech world, this is still done the old fashioned way. The duration of the eruption is clocked on a stopwatch. This information is figured into a chart to predict the next eruption time. From the visitor center, rangers estimate the height of the water column by comparing it to a tree that stands between the geyser and the visitor center. The height of the famous geyser has continued to average 130 feet since records have been kept.

After taking in the view, continue along the loop as it swings back around to the junction. Turn right here for a visit to another geyser with quite a different story. This path takes you through a shady forest past several seeps and springs— a cool, moist change from the hot exposed hilltop of Observation Point. The trail emerges at Solitary Geyser.

This geyser is appropriately named for its isolated location above Geyser Hill. Solitary was once a quiet and seldom visited hot spring, but in 1915, its waters were piped down to fill a swimming pool for visitors near the Old Faithful Inn. This lowered the water level and water pressure of this tranquil spring. Solitary Spring suddenly erupted as Solitary Geyser. The Old Faithful Geyser Bath House was closed in 1950, but this spring never returned to its original state. It continues to erupt every 4 to 8 minutes to a height of 4 to 15 feet. Though it didn't become a geyser naturally, enjoy the roiling eruption of this pretty spring, with its scalloped edges and terraced runoff channels.

The story of Solitary Geyser is one of human manipulation. Hopefully, it has taught us a lasting lesson. Geologists tell us that three things are required for geysers to erupt: water, heat, and a constricted plumbing system. Local rangers add a fourth condition to that list—preservation. While geysers exist in a number of places around the world, most have been harnessed for heat and energy. In Yellowstone, however, they are preserved for future generations to enjoy.

After visiting Solitary Geyser, take the trail that leads down to Geyser Hill. To return to the visitor center, take the boardwalk trail to the left until it rejoins the paved trail across the Firehole River. Promise yourself, however, to spend some time with the many geysers and hot springs of this world-renowned geyser basin.

25

This geyser stands alone in the forest,
but it has led many travelers to search for undiscovered geysers
in the most out-of-the-way places in the park.
—Geologist Arnold Hague, 1911

Lone Star Geyser

This is an excellent opportunity to observe a geyser without sharing the experience with hundreds of other people. Take this leisurely stroll along the Firehole River to one of Yellowstone's most predictable geysers. *See Plate 25.*

Level of difficulty: Moderate

Distance: 5 miles round trip (8 km)

Elevation change: Minimal

Duration: 2 - 3 hours

Best time of year: June to September.

Trailhead: This hike begins at the parking area 2.5 miles (4 km) southeast of the Old Faithful overpass on the south side of the Old Faithful–West Thumb Road, adjacent to Kepler Cascades.

Hiking directions: From the trailhead, hike south along the Firehole River. In 0.75 mile, the trail crosses a bridge and continues along the west side of the river. At the 1.6-mile mark, it passes the junction with the Spring Creek Trail on the left. Continue straight to Lone Star Geyser. To return, retrace your steps to the trailhead.

Special attention: If you'd like to see Lone Star Geyser erupt, it's worth checking at the Old Faithful Visitor Center for information on the last reported eruption. However, since the Lone Star area is not staffed, the rangers at Old Faithful may not have the most recent information. They depend on information given them from thoughtful hikers like you. Generally speaking though, with a 3 hour interval, eruptions often occur around the hours of 10:00 A.M., 1:00 P.M., and 4:00 P.M. At the geyser, check the log-book in which other hikers have recorded eruption times.

Naturalist notes: Before beginning your journey to Lone Star Geyser, take a moment to enjoy Kepler Cascades, which is located just west of the trailhead. Watch as the Firehole River falls 150 feet in a lovely cascade. On expedition here in 1870, Lt. Gustavus Doane wrote of it: *These pretty little falls if located on an east-*

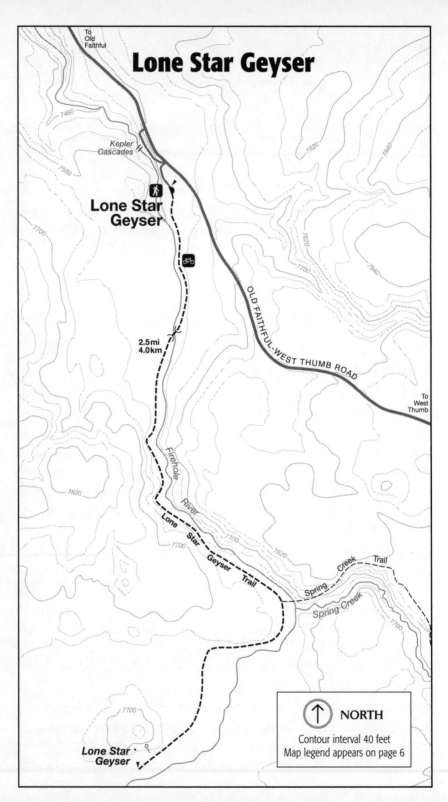

Lone Star Geyser

To
Old
Faithful

*Kepler
Cascades*

**Lone Star
Geyser**

2.5mi
4.0km

OLD FAITHFUL-WEST THUMB ROAD

To
West
Thumb

*Firehole
River*

Lone Star Geyser Trail

Spring Creek Trail

Spring Creek

*Lone Star
Geyser*

NORTH

Contour interval 40 feet
Map legend appears on page 6

ern stream would be celebrated in history and song; here amid objects so grand as to strain conception and stagger belief, they were passed without a halt.

After viewing the falls, walk alongside the parking area to the Lone Star Geyser Trailhead. The old road to the geyser is also a bike trail. Before 1972, you could drive to Lone Star, but the National Park Service closed the road to cars in that year to provide more paths for bicyclists.

For most of the way, you'll be following the Firehole River as it winds gently through the forest. At the beginning of the trail, however, you pass a small rapid on the river. This is the river that mountain man Jim Bridger said flowed so fast that friction made it hot. The Firehole is warm in places, but not for the reason that he suggests. One fourth of the river's flow is from thermal features farther downstream. There are also hot springs in the stream itself, making the bottom hot, as Bridger suggested.

Before long, the trail crosses the river on a cement bridge. Somewhere along the way, take time to sit down and enjoy the simple beauty of the river. Yellowstone provides a place of quiet retreat from the frenzied pace of life. You may find as the naturalist John Muir did on his travels:

The sun shines not on us, but in us. The rivers flow not past, but through us. The trees wave and the flowers bloom in our bodies as well as our souls, and every bird song, wind song, and tremendous storm song is our song...if only one is poor enough to listen.

Along the way, you'll be walking along the edge of a forest that varies between lodgepole pine, Engelmann spruce, and Douglas-fir. Though the fires raged near this area in 1988, high winds drove them over this small river valley.

Eventually, you'll meet the junction with the Spring Creek Trail that leads off to the left. Continue straight toward Lone Star Geyser. Had you been traveling this road in 1891, you'd have been on a stagecoach. The original road between Old Faithful and West Thumb turned left here at Spring Creek. Four horses would have pulled the coach on this, the most difficult leg of "the Grand Tour." The grade up Craig Pass was so steep that you'd have to get out and walk a few times to lighten the load on the horses. You'd be a little apprehensive here, because you'd have heard of several stagecoach robberies along this stretch of the road. The robbers were generally more greedy than they were dangerous, however. Some even posed to have their pictures taken. Most visitors considered it just a part of the Yellowstone experience! The Army completed the road on to Lone Star Geyser in 1895.

The river soon makes a wide meander to your left, away from the road, through a large meadow. Look for elk grazing here in the summer. Listen for them bugling in the fall during the annual ritual of the rut, or mating season. If you're lucky, you may hear the musical gargle of the sandhill cranes, which often feed in this meadow.

Long before a road existed here, the Hayden Survey of 1872 found their way through this dense forest to the geyser. The explorers named it Solitary Geyser because of its isolation from the other major geysers. Several years later, a park visitor named Joseph Cochran went hunting for a bear in the area. (Hunting was legal in the park at that time.) Unaware of the geyser, he saw a column of steam rising through the trees. Believing himself to be the first person to see it, he posted a sign naming it Lone Star Geyser. It's unknown why he gave it this name, though it appears to have no connection with Texas, the Lone Star State.

Upon reaching the geyser, cross the small footbridges over the runoff channels that will swell to full during an eruption. You'll see the massive cone of Lone Star Geyser, one of Yellowstone's largest, at 10 to 12 feet high. Position yourself well for this display of one of nature's rarest fountains. Lone Star is one of the most predictable geysers in the park, erupting about every three hours. With a few simple observations, you'll be able to predict when this geyser is about to go. An hour before an eruption, water begins to spout from one large vent and several smaller ones on the top of the cone. It may surge up to 45 feet several times in what are called minor eruptions. Don't leave yet. Soon, the geyser will go into full play, throwing a narrow jet of water 45 feet into the air for up to 30 minutes. The wind often blows the water into a curtain of mist, refracting a rainbow in the spray. After this impressive show, Lone Star goes into an exuberant steam phase.

Hundreds, maybe thousands of years ago, rain and snow fell in Yellowstone, beginning the process that would provide you with this performance today. Percolating down into the earth, this water was heated by hot rocks atop a magma chamber deep within the earth's crust. The superheated water then began to rise toward the surface through cracks and fissures in the ground. Since there was a constriction in the underground channels, pressure started to build. The weight of this pressure kept the water, which exceeded the boiling point, from flashing into steam. Bubbles eventually reached the surface, causing the geyser to overflow. This released the pressure on the water column and it started to boil violently. A huge volume of steam was produced, forcing water explosively out of the vent to create the terrific play you witness today.

If you'd like to assist others in predicting Lone Star, record the eruption time in the logbook near the geyser and report it to the ranger at the Old Faithful Visitor Center on your return.

This song of the waters is audible to every ear, but there is other music in these hills, by no means audible to all...sit quietly and listen.

–Naturalist Aldo Leopold

26

Mystic Falls &
Mystic Falls and Overlook

Convenient to Old Faithful, this short trail follows the Little Firehole River up a small canyon to a lovely 70-foot waterfall. For those wanting to hike a little farther, the trail climbs the Madison Plateau to an overlook offering superb views of the Upper Geyser Basin and the entire Old Faithful area. From this vantage point, you get an excellent perspective on the firestorm that rushed over this ridge on September 7, 1988. *See Plate 26.*

Mystic Falls

Level of difficulty: Easy

Distance: 2 miles round trip (3.2 km)

Elevation change: Minimal

Duration: 1 - 2 hours

Mystic Falls and Overlook

Level of difficulty: Moderate

Distance: 3-mile loop (4.8 km)

Elevation change: A gain of 500 feet in 0.5 mile

Duration: $1\frac{1}{2}$ - $2\frac{1}{2}$ hours

Best time of year: Mid-June through September. You may encounter snow on the ground when hiking this trail in spring and early summer, especially near the overlook.

Trailhead: This hike begins near Avoca Spring at the rear of Biscuit Basin, 2.1 miles north of the Old Faithful overpass on Old Faithful–Madison Road.

Hiking directions: From the parking area, the trail crosses a footbridge over the Firehole River and enters Biscuit Basin. At Avoca Spring, the Mystic Falls Trail leaves the boardwalk and heads into the forest. Soon you'll come to the Mystic

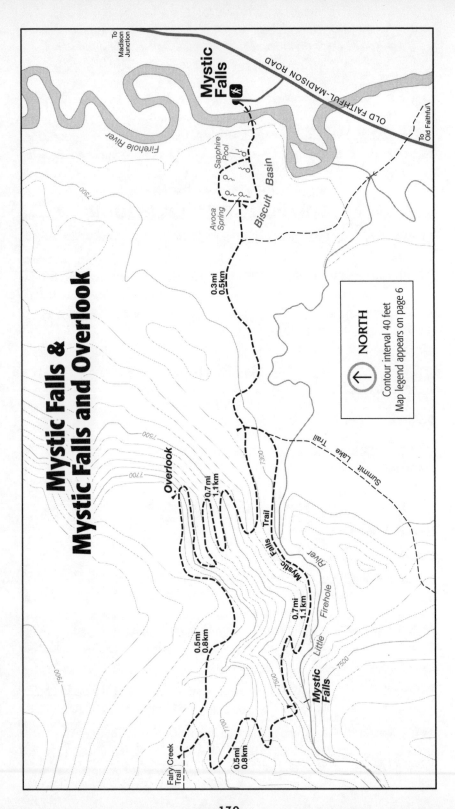

Mystic Falls & Mystic Falls and Overlook

To Madison Junction

Mystic Falls

OLD FAITHFUL-MADISON ROAD

To Old Faithful

Firehole River

Sapphire Pool

Avoca Spring

Biscuit Basin

0.3mi 0.5km

NORTH

Contour interval 40 feet
Map legend appears on page 6

7900

7500

7700

Overlook

0.7mi 1.1km

Summit Lake Trail

7300

Mystic Falls Trail

Little Firehole River

0.7mi 1.1km

7500

Mystic Falls

0.5mi 0.8km

7700

7900

7700

Fairy Creek Trail

0.5mi 0.8km

Falls Loop junction. Stay to the left. Soon, the trail intersects the Summit Lake Trail on the left. Continue straight, following the Little Firehole River 0.6 mile to the falls. For those wanting an easy hike, retrace your steps back to Biscuit Basin. Otherwise, continue on this loop trail to the overlook by climbing 500 feet in 0.5 mile over a series of switchbacks to where it meets the Fairy Creek Trail on the left. Follow the trail to the right for another 0.5 mile to the overlook. From here, the trail descends 0.7 mile on switchbacks to the Mystic Falls Loop junction. Heading straight, the trail returns to Biscuit Basin.

Special attention: Use caution when exploring around the bottom of Mystic Falls as a number of small hot springs are situated along the edge of the Little Firehole River.

Naturalist notes: As you cross the Firehole River, take a moment on the bridge to contemplate the lovely blue waters flowing beneath you. Here's an opportunity to become acquainted with one of the many rivers that weave through the Yellowstone landscape. Beyond the bridge, you enter onto a boardwalk trail that loops through Biscuit Basin. Home to geysers and hot springs, geologically this area is an extension of the Upper Geyser Basin. Sapphire Pool, the most prominent feature in this small thermal area, soon appears on the right.

What's less obvious today is the origin of the name Biscuit Basin. It was named for the large biscuit-shaped silica formations that once lined the edge of Sapphire Pool. In August 1959, the largest known earthquake in the Rocky Mountains struck just outside the park's western boundary. With a magnitude of 7.5, it brought about numerous changes in thermal activity throughout the park. Here, where you're standing, it triggered large eruptions of Sapphire Pool, blowing away the silica formations of this hot spring now turned geyser. Though the biscuits of Biscuit Basin are no more, the name is a telling reminder of the geologic change that constantly ripples through Yellowstone.

Ahead, the trail to Mystic Falls leaves the confines of the boardwalk near Avoca Spring. From here, you'll begin to travel through signs of more recent changes that touched this land—the fires of 1988. Passing a trail junction on the left, the trail continues straight, passing through a burned lodgepole pine forest with lots of standing dead snags and downed trees that have fallen since the fires burned this spot. Intermingled in this scene are several young lodgepoles, the next generation of Yellowstone forests.

Eventually, thoughts of the fires disappear as you begin to hear running water. When you reach the trail junction for the Mystic Falls Loop, take the path to your left. From here, the distance to the falls is 0.7 mile. Beyond this junction, the trail continues down a small hill and crosses the Summit Lake Trail on your left. Continue straight. Soon, the sound is revealed as the Little Firehole

River. With the river below the trail to your left, the Little Firehole and its many small rapids will be your hiking companion, leading you upstream to the falls. As you make your way up this small canyon, look for small hot spring seeps scattered around the river's edge lined with the distinctive yellow monkeyflower that seeks out these warmer waters. You may find elk in the grassy areas across the river.

As the trail bends to the right, the river's sound intensifies as you get your first glimpse of Mystic Falls. A few trails veer off the main path and scramble a few feet down to offer a better look. These trails to the river's edge are short and steep, but the view is well worth the effort. Tucked around the corner in the rocks are a number of small hot spring seeps scattered along the Little Firehole. Be careful, they're hot!

The trail climbs a few switchbacks to another fine view of the stately 70-foot Mystic Falls as it plunges in a series of steps off a narrow ledge of the Madison Plateau. On a cool day, steam can be seen rising from the top of the falls, indicating the presence of more thermal activity. With such interplay between hot and cold waters, this place is mystical indeed. The dictionary defines the word "mystic" in the spiritual realm—something that inspires a sense of wonder and surpasses understanding. Find a spot near the river in view of the falls. Watch the water ebb and flow, swirl and cascade as it tumbles on its merry way. Take the time to capture the wonder this little spot affords.

From here, you have a couple of choices. If you'd like to make this an easy hike, turn around, retracing your route along the Little Firehole River to Biscuit Basin. However, before turning back, you may wish to make the short climb up a few switchbacks toward the top of the falls, where you'll be treated to nice views looking downstream onto the Little Firehole and the Old Faithful area in the far distance.

For those desiring a longer outing and incredible views of the geyser basins, continue on this loop trail toward the overlook. The trail moves away from the falls and river as you ascend more switchbacks up the face of the Madison Plateau, a lava flow laid down in the wake of the Yellowstone caldera. About 0.5 mile and 500 feet later, you'll meet the Fairy Creek Trail, which takes off to the left. Stay to your right as the trail levels off and then loops back another 0.5 mile through rolling terrain amid thick stands of young lodgepoles. They offer excellent evidence of the regeneration since the fires.

As the trail arrives at the overlook, you're rewarded with the second highlight of this hike. Before you lies a view unlike any other on earth. From the edge of this lava flow, Biscuit Basin lies immediately below you. To your extreme right the Little Firehole River meanders toward Black Sand Basin.

Beyond, the Firehole River leads your eye to the Upper Geyser Basin, home of Old Faithful Geyser and the largest concentration of geysers in the world. From a similar vantage point, naturalist John Muir observed on a visit in 1885:

Looking down over the forests as you approach them from the surrounding heights, you see a multitude of white columns, broad,...irregular jets and puffs of misty vapor ascending from the bottom of the valley...So numerous they are and varied, Nature seems to have gathered them from all the world as specimens of her rarest fountains, to show in one place what she can do.

If you have the time to wait, take in an eruption of Old Faithful. You'll have the moment to yourself, even on the busiest of summer days.

In the far distance is the village of Old Faithful. From here, you have a sweeping view of forests, burned and unburned. Imagine the day, September 7, 1988, when a wall of fire driven by 70-mile-per-hour winds roared from this ridge down toward these buildings. Due to an heroic firefighting effort and the luck of a wind shift, all of the historically significant structures, including the Old Faithful Inn, were saved. From where you're standing, however, you can see how very close the fire came to destroying it.

Leaving the overlook, the trail descends 0.7 mile off the rock face through lodgepole pines and large Douglas-firs amid some interesting rocky outcrops before returning to the Mystic Falls Loop junction. Continue straight to retrace your steps back to Biscuit Basin.

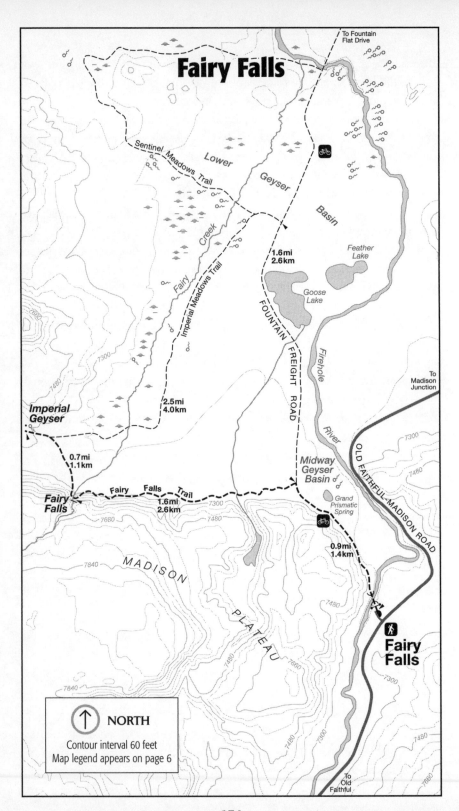

Fairy Falls

To Fountain
Flat Drive

Sentinel Meadows Trail

Lower

Geyser

Basin

Fairy

Creek

Imperial Meadows Trail

1.6mi
2.6km

Feather
Lake

Goose
Lake

FOUNTAIN FREIGHT ROAD

Firehole

River

To
Madison
Junction

2.5mi
4.0km

*Imperial
Geyser*

0.7mi
1.1km

*Midway
Geyser
Basin*

OLD FAITHFUL-MADISON ROAD

Fairy   Falls   Trail

**Fairy
Falls**

1.6mi
2.6km

*Grand
Prismatic
Spring*

0.9mi
1.4km

M A D I S O N

P L A T E A U

**Fairy
Falls**

NORTH

Contour interval 60 feet
Map legend appears on page 6

To
Old
Faithful

134

> *The fall proved upon measurement to be a clean descent of 250 feet, and dropped into a shallow and pretty basin at the foot by the cliff. I named this fall the Fairy.*
>
> —Captain John Whitney Barlow, 1871

27   PACK TRAIL

Fairy Falls

Travel along a historic road to the edge of a huge lava flow over which Fairy Falls plunges as a delicate 197-foot ribbon of water. From the falls, venture the short distance to the colorful waters of Imperial Geyser. On this trail, you'll see the regeneration of the forest since the fires of 1988. *See Plate 27.*

Level of difficulty: Moderate

Distance: 6.4 miles round trip (10.2 km)

Elevation change: Minimal

Duration: 3 - 4 hours

Best time of year: June through September. The Fairy Falls Trail is closed until the Friday of Memorial Day weekend as part of a bear management area.

Trailhead: This hike begins from the parking area for the Fairy Falls Trailhead on the west side of the road, 4.5 miles (7.2 km) north of the Old Faithful overpass and 11.5 miles (18.4 km) south of Madison Junction on the Old Faithful-Madison Road.

Hiking directions: From the parking area, pass the barricade and cross the steel bridge over the Firehole River. Begin hiking on the Fountain Freight Road, an historic route now open only to hikers and bicyclists. After 0.9 mile, the road meets the Fairy Falls Trail on the left. Turn left and hike 1.6 miles through a burned forest to Fairy Falls. From the falls, continue another 0.7 mile to Imperial Geyser. Return to the trailhead by the same route.

Special attention: Use caution when exploring around Imperial Geyser. Thermal areas have unstable ground with thin crust and scalding water.

Naturalist notes: This hike celebrates the beauty of water in all its forms, from rivers to geysers, to hot springs, to waterfalls. It begins at the Firehole River. This meandering stream is a unique blend of hot and cold water, with about a fourth of its flow composed of runoff from hot springs and geysers. With this thermal influence, the river stays ice-free all winter long, making it a haven for wintering wildlife. Enjoy the beauty of the river and the many thermal features and runoff channels near the trailhead as you cross the steel bridge and then begin hiking on an old wagon road. This historic route was built in 1883 by the Army Corps of Engineers as one of the first roads providing access to the geyser basins. Originally called National Park Avenue, it later became known as the Fountain Freight Road, a name that survives today. The road is no longer open to vehicles, only to hikers and bicyclists.

Follow the Fountain Freight Road as it parallels the edge of the Madison Plateau for the next 0.9 mile. Ahead, you'll see steam rising from Midway Geyser Basin. Once known as "Hell's Half Acre," Midway covers a relatively small area, but contains some of the park's largest thermal features, including Grand Prismatic Spring. At 370 feet across, it's Yellowstone's largest hot spring. Aptly named, it displays a spectrum of nature's loveliest hues. The brilliant yellows and oranges around the perimeter are a result of the bacteria that grow in the pool. Each color represents a different type of bacteria specialized to survive at a certain range of hot temperatures.

To fully appreciate Grand Prismatic, you must see it from above. If you're feeling ambitious, scramble up the burned ridge on your left to get a bird's-eye view. On any day, it's an impressive sight, but on a sunny day, the colors of the spring refracted in the rising steam create clouds of blue, red, orange, and green.

This scene has inspired many to record their impressions of this extraordinary hot spring. On her visit to Yellowstone in 1892, park visitor Georgina Synge observed:

This is a large pool called the Grand Prismatic Spring. Its surface is quite calm and unruffled, and its colors are indescribably lovely. In the center it is a wonderful dark deep blue, changing nearer the edge to a vivid green. Around the rim it fades into yellow— into orange—a ring of red -then purplish grey, the colors being intensified by the white coral-like deposit with which the pool is lined. One's eye revels in these glorious hues, as they melt one into another, the whole glistening in its pure white setting like a liquid jewel.

Ever the scientist, Ferdinand Hayden, leader of the first geological survey into the park in 1871, was nonetheless moved by what he saw at Grand Prismatic Spring: *Nothing ever conceived by human art could equal the peculiar vividness and delicacy of color of these remarkable prismatic springs. Life becomes a privilege and a blessing after one has seen and thoroughly felt these incomparable types of nature's cunning skill.*

Just past Grand Prismatic Spring, the road meets the trail to Fairy Falls. Turn left and continue to skirt the base of the Madison Plateau, a large lava flow laid down in the wake of Yellowstone's last enormous volcanic eruption 640,000 years ago. On the way to Fairy Falls, you'll pass through an area dramatically affected by the historic fires of 1988, when the North Fork Fire raged over the Madison Plateau, burning much in its path.

This stand of blackened trees was once a lodgepole pine forest—in fact, it still is, only changed. Growing beneath the standing dead trees is the next generation, a dense new forest of young trees. The lodgepole pine is uniquely adapted to fire by producing serotinous, or fire-dependent, cones, that can remain on a tree for years, sealed shut, protecting their seeds beneath a thin layer of resin. Such a cone will open only when the temperature exceeds 113° F, melting away the resin, thereby releasing its seeds. In 1988, shortly after the fires, fire ecologists found that, at some sites in Yellowstone, up to one million seeds per acre were deposited in this manner. If you look closely, you'll notice that some of these young lodgepoles already bear the cones that ensure their survival.

Ironically, then, it's only with fire that the lodgepole ensures its survival. During his visit to Yellowstone in 1885, naturalist John Muir observed this unique phenomenon and adaptation for survival:

...the lodgepole pine...takes pains to store up its seeds in firmly closed cones, and holds them [there]...so that, let the fire come when it may, it is ready to die and ready to live again in a new generation. For when the killing fires have devoured the leaves and thin resinous bark, many of the cones, only scorched, open as soon as the smoke clears away; the hoarded store of seeds is sown broadcast on the cleared ground, and a new growth immediately springs up triumphant out of the ashes. Therefore, this tree not only holds its ground, but extends its conquests farther after every fire.

Observing the natural processes at work has helped us to understand the role fire plays in maintaining an ecosystem. After a wildfire burns through older, sometimes diseased trees, a young and vibrant forest emerges. Lush grasses and flowers spring to life, drenched in sunshine from the exposed forest floor. Wildlife benefit from the profusion of new foods available, and so do we, as we're now able to see into these open spaces and observe the animals grazing there. As you hike, enjoy the many new grasses and flowers blooming each summer in this soil enriched by ash. Near the falls, you may notice the burned forest changes from lodgepole to more spruce and fir. Without the benefit of the serotinous cone, fewer young trees are growing here. Given time, the forest will return.

In the end, the historic fires of 1988 provided many valuable lessons regarding the interrelationship between forest and fire as well as to our own relationship to this often misunderstood and feared force of nature.

Down the trail, you'll soon hear the sound of rushing water as the picturesque Fairy Falls comes into view. Well worth the journey, this 197-foot falls is one of the park's tallest waterfalls and definitely one of its loveliest. On its way to the Firehole River, the waters of Fairy Creek fall gracefully over the edge of the Madison Plateau. The water spills along the face of the rock in an almost slow-motion dance. Then it collects in a quiet pool at the base of the falls. This cool and refreshing spot is the ideal place for a picnic lunch. As mist from the falls swirls in the air, enjoy the beauty of these falling waters.

The trail continues 0.7 mile beyond the falls, following Fairy Creek for a short while, before leading you to water in a different form—geysers. On the way, notice a different species of tree appearing in the burned forest. Aspens are growing in profusion, struggling mightily to grow beyond the reach of elk who browse on them. Since the fires, scientists have found aspen growing from seed, rather than by cloning, a phenomenon they have never seen before. The wonders of Yellowstone, even amid fires, never cease.

In a short distance, the trail crosses a wetland and meets the junction with the Imperial Meadows Trail. Stay to your left as the trail passes through a dense thicket of young lodgepoles. Billowing steam will lead you to Imperial Geyser, which soon appears prominently on your right. Tucked beneath the glacially deposited rock forming the Twin Buttes, this feature, when active, erupts from a beautiful blue pool 100 feet wide.

Imperial Geyser has an interesting history. It was first seen erupting in 1927 by scientists Allen and Day. Fascinated by what they had found, they undertook an extensive study of this newest geyser, bringing much notoriety to the feature. In 1929, as a means of promoting the park, National Park Service founder and Director Stephen Mather hosted a conference at Old Faithful for newspapers from around the country. Mather invited those in attendance to vote on a name for this new geyser. The most popular choices were "Imperial" and "Columbia," with Imperial emerging as the winner.

The name was a good choice, for in its day it was truly regal. Between 1927 and 1929, Imperial was one of Yellowstone's most significant geysers, erupting for periods of 4 to 6 hours to heights of 80 to 150 feet. At its peak, each eruption of Imperial discharged almost 900,000 gallons of water, among the greatest output of any feature in the park. Sadly, Imperial fell silent in late 1929, remaining quiet until it experienced a rejuvenation in 1966. In recent years, it has shown some signs of life. If you're interested in learning more about the current activity of Imperial, inquire at the Old Faithful Visitor Center.

When you've finished exploring the thermal area around Imperial Geyser, return to Fairy Falls and retrace your route back to the trailhead.

If you'd like to take a longer route back through some open meadows, consider the following loop. Hiking this loop will add an additional 1.8 miles to the trip, bringing the total distance to 8.2 miles. Retrace your route from Imperial

Geyser to where it meets the Imperial Meadows Trail. Veer left here, instead of heading back to Fairy Falls. This trail will take you through open meadows bounding Fairy Creek across the Lower Geyser Basin. In about 2.2 miles the trail rejoins the Fountain Freight Road. To complete the loop, turn right and follow the road 1.6 miles past Goose Lake and along the Firehole River to where you rejoin the trail to Fairy Falls. Continue straight on the Fountain Freight Road another 0.9 mile to return to the trailhead.

The contents [of the mudpots]...were of the consistency of thick paint...
The bubbles would explode with a puff, emitting...a villainous smell.

—Explorer Nathaniel Langford, 1870

28

Artists' Paintpots

Of all Yellowstone's "geothermal curiosities," the mudpots seem to be among the most memorable. If you'd like to see bubbling pots of splattering mud, this is where you'll find them. Located on Paintpot Hill, the mudpots are surrounded by a palette of colorful hot springs. *See Plate 28.*

Level of difficulty: Easy

Distance: 1 mile round trip (1.6 km)

Elevation change: 100 feet

Duration: 45 minutes - 1 hour

Best time of year: June through September

Trailhead: This hike begins from a side road on the east side of the main road, 3.8 miles (6.1 km) south of Norris Junction and 9.9 miles (15.9 km) north of Madison Junction on the Madison-Norris Road. From the turn-off, the side road continues 0.2 mile to the trailhead.

Hiking directions: From the parking area, follow the boardwalk through the forest for 0.6 mile until it reaches the thermal area. Turn left at this junction. A short loop trail climbs Paintpot Hill. After making the loop, retrace your steps to the trailhead.

Special attention: Keep a safe distance from the thermal features. Watch for mud splattering over the railings.

Naturalist notes: This colorful escapade begins in a sea of green. The trail takes you through the young forest that has emerged since the fires of 1988 burned through here with a vengeance, filling the sky with orange flames and leaving everything behind them, black. The density of the trees speaks to the powerful regenerative forces brought on by fire.

The forest opens up into several clearings before the trail reaches Paintpot Hill, which looms before you in the distance. In these clearings, you'll find lodgepole pines that didn't burn, but had the misfortune to grow too near or be overtaken by, thermal waters. The curious white bands around the bottom of the trees

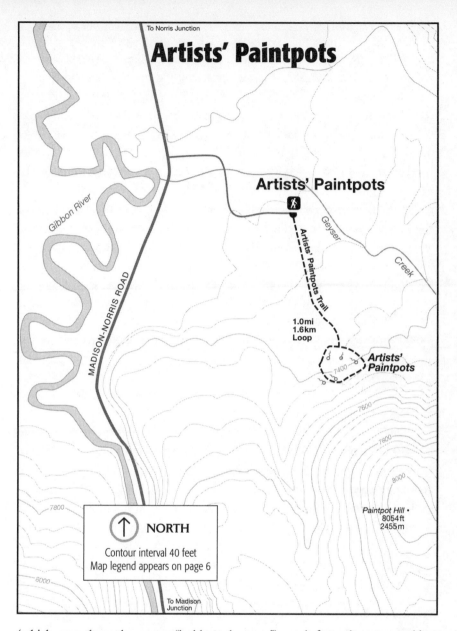

Map legend appears on page 6

(which gave them the name, "bobbysocks trees") result from the trees soaking up water containing a light colored mineral called silica. Needing fresh water to survive, not this mineral laden therman soup, the lodgepoles eventually die. Don't get off the trail to investigate. These thermal waters wouldn't do you any good either!

Soon, you'll reach the boardwalk trail at the thermal basin. At the loop junction, turn left, and cross over a small thermal creek. At the base of Paintpot Hill, the trail veers left again and starts to climb. But before you start to climb too, pause by the hot spring at the bend in the trail and take time to enjoy the two small geysers there. The nearest to the trail, brilliantly red in color, splashes boisterously to a maximum height of 6 feet. This small but mighty geyser has erupted continually since it was first recorded in 1926. It's what geologists call a "perpetual spouter." Don't let its diminutive size deceive you. This geyser discharges up to 150 gallons of water per minute! To the right of this feature is another small geyser. Difficult to see from the trail, its vent is a crack in a boulder. The small pool pulsates constantly, throwing water up to 4 feet in the air.

As the trail climbs Paintpot Hill, look and listen for steam hissing along the way. These features are referred to as "fumaroles." Gasses rush forcefully from vents in the earth here. If there was water available, these features would be roiling hot springs. In fact, a good rainfall will transform them into just that. Fumaroles are the most changeable of the thermal features. Oddly enough, these dry features are surrounded by moist ground, sporting water-loving ferns.

As you gain elevation up Paintpot Hill, you'll also gain great views of the prominent peaks of the Gallatin Range: Mount Holmes, Dome Mountain, and Trilobite Point. Mount Holmes was named for an early explorer in the area. Imagine what it must have been like to come across a place such as this. You're about to discover, for yourself, some of the mudpots for which Yellowstone is famous.

Mudpots seem to be what many people remember most from their visit to the park. It's not hard to understand why. Perhaps they bring back that childlike sense of wonder many of us have long since forgotten. An elderly visitor to the park in 1922 called this area "perfect heaven for mud-pie makers." Her companions noticed that she was "growing younger every mile" on her journey through Yellowstone. Several mud cones lead the way to the star performer. Watch its bubbles slowly build and bulge until they burst up to 15 feet high. Be careful: sometimes they throw hot mud over the railings! Listen to them gurgle and blurp and spit and splatter. It's great to be a kid again!

Explorer Nathaniel Langford had to use his imagination to describe these somewhat indescribable features: *The contents…were of the consistency of thick paint…boiling much after the fashion of a hasty pudding in the last stages of completion. The bubbles…would explode with a puff, emitting each time, a villainous smell.…*

That "villainous" smell tells of how these curious and delightful features are formed. Hydrogen sulfide gas, the cause of the rotten egg smell, exists deep in the earth's crust. It works its way up from its deep origins, mixing with water along the way. The combination of the two creates a weak form of sulfuric acid. This acid dissolves the rock at the surface, turning it into thick viscous mud. Carbon dioxide, steam, and hydrogen sulfide gasses explode through the mud in the whimsical bursting bubbles that entertain you today. Can anyone resist smiling at these sights and sounds?

After enjoying a bit of a second childhood, follow the trail down the hill and continue around the loop as it parades past a number of hot springs that span the spectrum. It's almost as if this could be the palette from which some master painter created the colorful canvas of Yellowstone.

The scientist in you will be interested to discover that the reddish color in the pools is the result of the presence of iron oxide minerals. The yellow, orange, brown, and green colors result from the algae and bacteria that grow in thermal waters. The artist in you will simply enjoy the beauty of the scene.

When you reach the loop junction, turn left and retrace your steps back to the trailhead—but not before promising yourself to try your hand at a few watercolors yourself, like you always wanted to do as a kid.

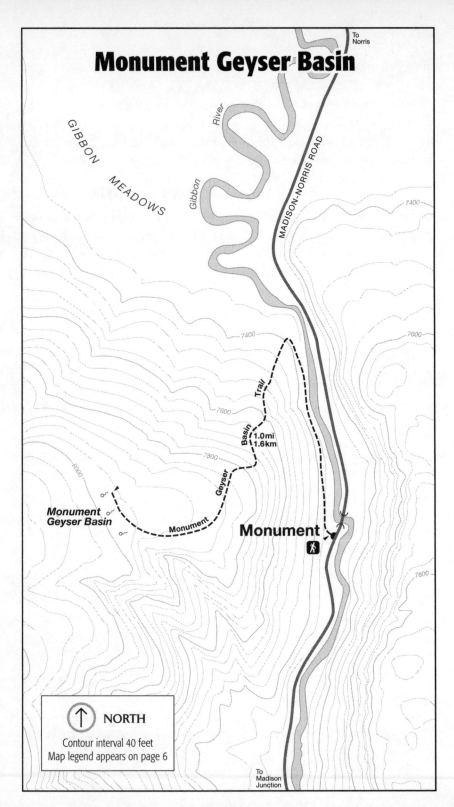

Monument Geyser Basin

To Norris

Gibbon River

Gibbon

GIBBON MEADOWS

MADISON-NORRIS ROAD

7400

7600

7400

Basin Trail

7600

1.0mi
1.6km

7800

Geyser

8000

Monument
Geyser Basin

Monument

Monument

7800

7600

To
Madison
Junction

↑ NORTH

Contour interval 40 feet
Map legend appears on page 6

*[Here is]…a deposit of hot springs, strongly suggesting
the work of human hands; some ancient memorial to the dead
in this remote and secluded spot.*
—Scientists Allen and Day, 1935

Monument Geyser Basin

This short but very steep trail takes you to a small thermal area filled with a collection of odd looking, yet strangely beautiful geyser cones, unlike any others found in the park. At the top await great views of the Gibbon River Canyon, Gibbon Meadows, and the Gallatin Range. Along the way, you'll have the opportunity to witness the forest's rebirth in the wake of the great fires of 1988. *See Plate 29.*

Level of difficulty: Moderate

Distance: 2 miles round trip (3.2 km)

Elevation change: A gain of 640 feet in 0.6 mile

Duration: $1\frac{1}{2}$ - 2 hours

Best time of year: Mid-June through September.

Trailhead: This hike begins from the pullout at the Gibbon River Bridge on the west side of the road, 5 miles (8 km) south of Norris Junction and 9 miles (14.4 km) north of Madison Junction on the Madison-Norris Road.

Hiking directions: From the trailhead, follow the river upstream for about 0.4 mile. The trail bends sharply to the left and climbs a very steep hillside, 640 feet in 0.6 mile, to the geyser basin. Explore along the edge of the thermal area, then return to the trailhead by the same route.

Special attention: Monument Geyser Basin is a fragile thermal area containing unstable ground with thin crust and scalding water. For your safety and to ensure the protection of these delicate features, do not go near them. Although the trail is short, it's strikingly steep. Sturdy hiking boots are recommended.

Naturalist notes: The hike to Monument Geyser Basin begins deceptively easily. Along this level part of the trail, you'll immediately begin to notice an assortment of hot springs and steam vents, called "fumaroles," across the Gibbon River. About one-fifth of this river is thermal runoff. This hot water hints at what lies ahead.

From the lovely stone bridge spanning the river, hike upstream along the water's edge for 0.4 mile. Along the way, enjoy the sounds and comfort the river provides as it begins to pick up speed after leaving Gibbon Meadows.

From its origins at Grebe Lake in the Washburn Range, the Gibbon River follows a course that leads to Madison Junction, where it joins with the Firehole River. This confluence gives birth to the larger Madison River, which flows from Yellowstone as one branch of the headwaters of the Missouri. As you hike, you may notice fishermen plying the waters of the Gibbon. Popular with anglers, the river is home to a number of introduced species including brook, brown, and rainbow trout, in addition to the native cutthroat and grayling.

The name Gibbon was first given to the river by members of the second Hayden Geological Survey in 1872, in honor of General John Gibbon, a civil war officer who later served on the western frontier in the Montana Territory. Gibbon had explored a portion of this watercourse during a visit to Yellowstone in the park's first year. As a result, Frank Bradley noted in the Hayden Survey's annual report to Congress: *As this stream has been partially explored by General Gibbon, who gave us some useful information concerning it, we have called it Gibbon's Fork of the Madison.*

Soon, the trail bends to the left, following the river as it emerges from Gibbon Meadows, home to elk, bison, and an occasional coyote or sandhill crane. Through the meadows, the river winds lazily in a series of sweeping meanders and oxbow bends. This hike, however, has other things in mind. The trail takes a extreme turn to the left, bending back away from the river and immediately beginning its rigorous climb. For the next 0.6 mile, the trail ascends a steep hill, gaining 640 feet in short order. As it does, it passes through an extensive area of burned forest. Rest often as you make your way up, taking time to investigate the changes that have occurred here since the 1988 fires swept across this ridge. Enjoy the numerous wildflowers and grasses that cover the ground in the now-sunny soils previously shaded by a dense canopy of trees. Sprinkled beneath the standing parent trees are the young lodgepoles that have grown out of the fertile ash bed the fire provided. After the hike, as you drive the road between Madison and Norris, you'll notice thousands more of these new trees born of fire, representing the next generation of the forest.

Just before you reach the Geyser Basin, you get a remarkable view to the south. The Gibbon River no longer wanders quietly. With heightened purpose, it churns in a series of rapids carving the narrow Gibbon River Canyon. Beyond this scenic chasm, as far as you can see, layer after layer of lava flows stretch out to form the broad Yellowstone Plateau. You're looking into an area where, 640,000 years ago, one of the earth's most powerful volcanic eruptions occurred. At that time, magma welled up within the crust, causing a massive volcano to erupt and then collapse, leaving a huge caldera, or depression, in the earth's surface. Since then, successive lava flows have filled the caldera, leaving this expansive volcanic plateau that covers much of central Yellowstone. Notice that there are no mountains here. Perhaps the Gallatins to the northwest once extended farther south into where the caldera is now. Geologists will never really know, as the explosion and subsequent collapse of the earth's surface either blew away or consumed whatever was in its path. What's left today is a unique landscape, atypical of the Rocky Mountains.

Farther ahead, the trail arrives at Monument Geyser Basin amid incredible views and the smell of sulfur. To the north, Gibbon Meadows stretch out beneath you, the wide meanders of the river clearly visible from this vantage point. Beyond the basin to the northwest rises the southern extent of the Gallatin Range, with Mount Holmes quite prominent. The Washburn Range comprises the mountainous terrain in the far distance to the northeast.

Poised just north of the caldera boundary and sitting within one of these lava flows, the Monument Geyser Basin is a constant reminder of the park's explosive past. In this long narrow basin, the air is filled with the smell of rotten eggs as sulfur cauldrons and fumaroles bubble and hiss. Adding to this otherworldly appearance is a collection of strange looking geyser cones. Over time, the silica in the water erupting from these features has slowly been deposited to create some very unique cones. Unfortunately, all but one of these geysers are now dormant, having sealed themselves up. The one feature still showing a little sign of life is the basin's namesake, Monument Geyser. Also known as Thermos Bottle Geyser, it's 10 feet tall and looks like its name suggests. Not quite yet sealed over, it mostly steams and sprays a little water.

Through the years, people have conceived of the most unusual images in these sinter (formed of silica) cones, giving them names like the Sunning Seal, the Dog's Head, and the Sperm Whale. What does your imagination see in these fanciful creations?

When you're done exploring nature's own sculpture garden, hike back to the trailhead via the same route.

Index

About the authors

Roger Anderson and Carol Shively Anderson have been rangers with the National Park Service in four different parks since 1980, and have over 35 years combined service in Yellowstone National Park. Their work has primarily been in education, sharing the values of these treasured places with people from all over the world. They also have experience in research, resource management, and wildland firefighting. Carol currently manages interpretive services in the Lake Area of Yellowstone. Roger manages cultural resources for the park and is the editor of the park's quarterly journal, *Yellowstone Science*.